Y0-BSQ-227

The CONVERT and the COUNSELLOR

Okey Onuzo, M.D.

10,000 copies — First Edition
SECOND EDITION

To all those who came to Christ through my witness, whom I never got to share with in person.

SECOND EDITION

All rights reserved. No part of this publication may be reproduced, stored in a retrieval system, or transmitted, in any form or by any means, electronic, mechanical, photocopying, recording, or otherwise, without the prior written permission of the author.

Copyright © 1990 by Dr. Okey Onuzo
ISBN 1-880608-00-6

Published by Life Link Worldwide, Inc.
350 Marley Drive, College Park, Ga. 30349

Worldwide Distribution
NIGERIA - Life Publication
1, Oba Docemo Street
G.R.A. Ikeja, Lagos, NIGERIA.

Printed in the United States of America

ε.24
c

L. I. F. E Bible College
LIBRARY
1100 COVINA BLVD
SAN DIMAS, CA 91773

CONTENTS

043968

Foreword

The church in Africa has experienced an explosion in terms of numbers, in the last fifty years. Perhaps, the immediate past twenty-five years are the most dramatic. Nigeria has had its fair share in this harvest of souls and has probably become the first country ever, where the swing of the pendulum is actually turning from a non-Christian majority to a greater Christian population.

However, the turn-over of those who "make decisions" has also been quite alarming.

As someone who has been in church leadership at various levels for the last 30 years, I strongly affirm that this book, *The Convert and the Counsellor* by Dr. Okey Onuzo, is one that is both timely and relevant. Reading through it for me has been quite an experience.

The move of the Holy Spirit in our times has been so all pervading that hardly any class of persons has been left untouched. The result is that most of our follow-up material prepared years ago, have been out of step with the intensity and the quality of thought that go with the current generation, more especially the wide spectrum of elites who are making personal encounters with the living Christ.

Dr. Okey Onuzo's style of writing is quite original and innovative. What he shares is intensely personal and well balanced. He is very down-to-earth and practical. One set back I notice is that Okey does not claim to know everything nor have all the answers. But that perhaps is the greatest strength of the book, for at the end, you wonder, 'what is left?'

Let me leave you with three warnings:

1. Don't attempt to read this book in a hurry; in fact you cannot. So, take your time.

2. Don't be afraid to discover that once you commence reading, you will find it difficult to give up.

3. Don't be surprised to feel by the time you conclude, that you cannot really say you have 'finished' the book. You need to go over it again and again, and refer to it from time to time.

I commend the book to the *Evangelist* who goes about sowing the seed. I commend the book to the *Pastor* whose duty it is to care for the convert. I commend the book to the *Counsellor* whose hand has been immensely strengthened by this invaluable tool. I commend the book to the *Convert* who is the prime target of the work. Finally, to God our Father, who has willed that none should perish, I commend *The Convert and the Counsellor*.

DR. SAMUEL O. ODUNAIKE

Member, Lausanne Committee for World Evangelisation

Introduction

The subject matter of follow-up is a basic problem plaguing all our efforts to reach the unsaved for the kingdom of God not only here in Nigeria, but all over the world. These efforts find expression in our revival meetings, crusades, breakfast and dinner meetings.

That this subject is of utmost importance could be seen from what the Apostle Paul told his evangelistic team in Acts of the Apostles chapter 15, verse 36: "And some days after, Paul said unto Barnabas, Let us go again and visit our brethren in every city where we have preached the word of the Lord, and see how they do".

Preaching the gospel is a mandate to the Church. But on its own, it would be incomplete without follow-up of those who respond positively to the message of salvation in Christ Jesus.

This is the purpose of this book.

It is a down-to-earth counsel for the new convert who has just been born into the kingdom of God, and needs direction and support in this dark and confused world.

It is also an appropriate manual for the counsellor who is faced with the awesome task of following-up young converts.

Having been a Christian for about two decades, and by virtue of the various positions he has held in the Body of Christ, our beloved brother is in a good position to know who is a convert and what a counsellor should be saying to him.

I sincerely and prayerfully recommend this book to the body of Christ universal, and to every individual who is sincere about the task of world evangelisation.

Pastor E. A. Adeboye

General Overseer, The Redeemed Christian Church of God, Ebute-Metta, Lagos - Nigeria.

Preface to Second Edition

The first edition of this book released in July 1990, had a global reception that went beyond our wildest imagination. Given the obstacles facing a relatively unknown writer particularly overseas, it was amazing to see how reader after reader in Nigeria, Europe and the United States of America testified to the usefulness of the book in meeting its set objective, which is to provide a handy material for converts and their counsellors, and so assist young believers to settle down in their faith with minimal delay.

It is no wonder then that the initial ten thousand copies printed have been used up by individuals, organisations and ministries as well as by churches.

We thank the Lord each week when we hear of someone whose life was touched by the book. There was this lady who had felt this intense urge to read the book just before a job interview, and went in to find that the first question she was asked was to explain what it meant to be born again. A business executive here in Lagos was ready for believer's baptism after reading the book. There was the Pastor in Providence Rhode Island USA, who gave copies to his converts to Christ. One of them was so blessed that she insisted on thanking the author in person.

This second edition has undergone extensive stylish modification. The material content has remained essentially unchanged except for some more information on personal witnessing, and the Baptism of the Holy Ghost.

My prayer remains that the good Lord will continue to use *The Convert and the Counsellor* as a tool for this end-time harvest, in Jesus name, Amen.

Dr. Okey Onuzo

Preface to First Edition

I must thank the Lord for helping me to lay down this burden that had been on my mind. I have felt the need to write a short material like this to hand over to the converts after all those meetings the Lord has enabled me to hold in several places.

You know how the preacher always leaves the follow-up to the organisers, admonishing the young converts to attend the local counselling sessions. It has been frustrating each time we check the number of converts against the number that attended the new converts class, or against the number that eventually stayed back in fellowship. The truth which we discovered is that many of the converts are lost to follow-up.

As president of the FULL GOSPEL BUSINESS MEN'S FELLOWSHIP INTERNATIONAL, Ikeja chapter in Lagos, Nigeria, I was very much aware that our staying result was less than 40%. In fact if we had anything near 30%, we would literally be bursting in the seams. We had as many as 200 converts in one breakfast outreach at one time, and each outreach meeting records a minimum of forty converts to Christ.

As a Field Representative of the FGBMFI in the Lagos area, I see the problem in a wider context.

Following up young converts in Lagos in particular poses a tremendous challenge. There are enough communication obstacles to frustrate even the most ambitious counsellor. Thank God for all those faithful men and women who trace out each convert's address in their neighbourhood, and pay them that crucial visit.

In my local church here in Nigeria, the home-based Fellowship Centres, called Life Centres do a great work of reaching the converts in their neighbourhoods. In spite of all that monumental effort, the staying percentage is still less than 30%, given the number of converts that kneel at the altar every Sunday service.

These are the factors that created this burden to produce this material, which I pray the Holy Spirit of God will use to help more and more people to stay with their confession of faith in Christ Jesus, as Lord and Saviour, Amen.

What I have done here is to simulate the dialogue at the home of a young convert during an initial follow-up visit by a counsellor, who now attempts to assist the convert to better appreciate his or her recent experience of the new birth, its scope, and its implications to his or her day to day life.

Dr. Okey Onuzo

Preamble

On June 28th 1970, I attended a meeting at the city of Enugu organised by the Scripture Union Group there. I went there merely to find out for myself what they were really saying about being born again.

At the end of that meeting, or rather before I finally left that meeting hall, I had signed a piece of paper to indicate that I had given my life to Christ. That meant I was born again. Nobody told me in that meeting what was supposed to have happened to me. Nobody told me in any detail what to expect. That would be too much to ask of a preacher in a thirty minute to forty-five minute sermon.

The good Lord touched my heart, and drew me to Himself. That was what happened on the day that I was born again.

As a lay-minister of God over the years, one of the greatest problems that I have encountered is how to ensure that all those who answer the "altar call" to give their hearts to Jesus are adequately followed-up so they can be firmly established in Christ, rooted and grounded in the truth in God's word.

A professional colleague of mine who is also a lay-minister of God once told me of a young lady who was soliciting on one of the highways in a certain city here in Nigeria. The gentleman that she approached declined her overtures, and explained to her that as a born again child of God, he could not indulge in such escapades anymore. The lady shocked him by saying that she too was born again, but that circumstances beyond her control had forced her to take to the streets.

Follow up is a basic duty of Christians. This book is not designed to eliminate those house calls that are so useful in confirming the faith of the young convert to Christ. It is not meant to make us all sit home and simply pray that they will use the book. It will never replace those calls where we share from the depths of our hearts how we came to love the Lord so much so that nothing else has mattered that much ever since. It is there that we dare to confide that things were not always this way with us. We stop to open our hearts to share our struggles and our victories, as well as the times we had failed. Nothing can replace those person to person interaction that mean so much to the young convert.

I believe what the Holy Ghost wants me to do here is see if by His grace I can be used to produce what you can leave behind with the young believer. Something additional to your visit. Something he or she can refer to for consolidation after you have gone. Some kind of reference support if you like.

There is no way a book like this can be exhaustive. It is not designed to be. It is simply an addition to our usual house calls after a soul has moved from the kingdom of darkness into the Kingdom of Light, the kingdom of God.

Sources of bible quotations

GNB - Good News Bible

KJV - King James Version

NKJ - New King James Version

LB - Living Bible

NIV - New International Version

RSV - Revised Standard Version

Convert.......Sans serif typeface (Helvetica)
Counsellor....Serifed typeface (Times Roman)

Chapter One

UNDERSTANDING THE NEW BIRTH EXPERIENCE

What is it all about?

The phrase born again was used by our Lord Jesus Christ in His discussions with the Jewish leader, Nicodemus. This you may find in the Gospel of John chapter 3 from verses 1 to 7. I think you should get your Bible and read the passage.

What may strike you there is the emphasis, particularly in verses 3, 5, and 7.

"Jesus answered and said unto him, Verily, verily, I say unto thee, Except a man be born again, he cannot see the kingdom of God."

He repeatedly emphasized that an individual *must* be born again. So you can see that what you have just done is something that Jesus says you just must do if you want to enter into the kingdom of God.

So you might say that the new birth is the gateway into the kingdom of God. Let us put it this way: A person that is coming into this world, has to be born into it. There is no other way to come. Similarly, a person going into the kingdom of God is also born into it. There is just no other way to go in.

What does it really mean?

The best way to answer that question is to look closely at verse 6 of John chapter 3.

> "That which is born of the flesh is flesh; and that which is born of the Spirit is spirit."

The implication of this passage is that an individual undergoes two kinds of birth. One is physical, the other is spiritual. Obviously the physical precedes the spiritual.

I suppose what one should really ask is what it means to be born spiritually. To be able to answer that question properly, I believe we should touch on some fundamental issues relating to a man's relationship with God. Two of these are quite important. The first is the nature of man; the second is the fall of man. Let us take them one by one.

The Nature of Man

We gain some useful insight into the nature of man at the time he was created by the Almighty God from Genesis chapter 2 and verse 7.

> "And the Lord God formed man of the dust of the ground, and breathed into his nostrils the breath of life; *and man became a living soul.*"

When the Bible says that man was formed of the dust of the earth, I believe it is referring to human anatomy or structure, and human physiology and biochemistry or function. Simply put, a man is very close to nature because he is made of the same minerals that can be found in the soil around us. This is why a man's body decays at death and returns to dust again providing food for plants and other types of living things.

After God formed the body from the minerals in the soil, that body had no life in it until the Spirit of God referred to here as God's breath of life, entered it.

When the Spirit of Life, the Spirit of God touched that lifeless body, the man became conscious or aware. The Bible says he started from the moment of that contact to have a soul.

So we may conclude that a man has three parts to him: his *body*, his *soul*, and his *spirit*.

There are times some people find it difficult to tell the difference between the soul and the spirit of man. The way to understand it is to separate them into three, with respect to their origins. The body came from the earth. The spirit came from God. The soul on the other hand is the result of the impact of the Spirit on the lifeless body of man. It exists in the human conscious-ness and it manifests in three key areas: the will, the intellect, and the emotion.

It is important to bear the nature of man in mind because it helps us to understand the fall of man.

The Fall of Man

One thing we learn about the creation of man is that God wanted him to be in charge of the earth. This is the way He put it to them in Genesis chapter 1 and verse 28.

"And God blessed them, and God said unto them, Be fruitful, and multiply, and replenish the earth, and subdue it: and have dominion over the fish of the sea, and over the fowl of the air, and over every living thing that moveth upon the earth." [KJV]

Because man was in charge for God, He made a covenant with him, which is a kind of contract. He put a tree in the garden where the man and his wife were living merely to symbolize that covenant or agreement. What that covenant says in essence is that God is truly the one in charge; man is only in charge on God's behalf. This is why the tree that symbolized that agreement was called The Tree of the Knowledge of Good and Evil. *Man was not to determine good and evil for himself. Things should be good or evil, depending on how God had labelled them.* This is how He put it to the man in Genesis chapter 2 and verses 16 and 17.

"And the Lord God commanded the man, saying, Of every tree of the garden thou mayest freely eat:

But of the tree of the knowledge of good and evil, thou shalt not eat of it: for in the day that thou eatest thereof thou shalt surely die." [KJV]

The key to understanding the fall of man is in that statement that denotes the consequences of failure to comply: *thou shalt surely die.*

You may need to read Genesis chapter 3 and verses 1 to 19 in order to get the whole picture. To cut a long story short. The devil convinced the man and his wife to eat fruit from this tree. Consequent on this disobedience, they died, but not physically. They died spiritually. What this means really is that they lost the indwelling presence of the Spirit of God and as a result of that, their human spirit became non-functional.

When Jesus referred to spiritual birth in John chapter 3, as the gateway into the kingdom of God, He meant that the Spirit of God must return to dwell in anyone who seeks to share eternity with God.

It is important to also note that when the Spirit of God departed from man, thereby rendering his human spirit non-functional, he began to live according to the dictates of his soul. What this really means practically is that man started to act, not as God wills any longer, but according to the way he wills, thinks or feels. I am sure you can identify with that in your everyday life. I certainly can.

Let us then conclude by saying that what happens when a person is born again is that the Spirit of God comes into him, quickens his human spirit and dwells with him.

It is this quickened human spirit that enables the individual to communicate with the Spirit of God now dwelling within him. Subsequent to that, the capacity to live as God wills, is again restored, as the human spirit and the Spirit of God resume communion or dialogue.

Please explain the new birth process again

Indeed one may be born again, but may never really be able to explain how it all happened, or for that matter why it had to be that way.

I think it is helpful to know some of the consequences of the fall of man. The one key thing that happened is that when the man decided to choose good and evil by himself, he inherited the nature of evil, call it the tendency to choose evil rather than good. You may define evil as something or anything that is outside of what God has said. Because of that choice to do what God has not said, man then started to choose mostly what God has not ordered. This tendency to choose evil rather than good is universal. There is no one who does not have to fight to do what is right. What is wrong is often easier. This is what the Bible means in Romans chapter 3 and verse 23, where it says:

"For all have sinned, and come short of the glory of God." [KJV]

God has a law with regard to sin. That law is stated clearly in Ezekiel chapter 18, verse 4. It may also be found in Romans chapter 6 and verse 23. You may check these out now, but here is what they say:

"Behold, all souls are mine; as the soul of the father, so also the soul of the son is mine: *the soul that sinneth, it shall die.*" [Ezekiel 18:4 KJV]

"For the wages of sin is death..." [Romans 6 :23a]

You will agree with me that if God were to carry out this law to the letter, there will be nobody left on the surface of the earth. So what God did was to provide man with a substitute. You may read about all these in the book of Leviticus, particularly chapters 3, 5, 6, 7, and 17.

Essentially there are two types of offerings prescribed. One is the peace offering when a man seeks reconciliation with God, and the other is the trespass offering or the sin offering.

With the peace offering, a man brings the substitute animal, and lays his hand on the head of the animal, before the priest offers it as a sacrifice on the altar. The blood of that animal is the symbol of the life that has been given as a substitute for the sinner.

With the sin or trespass offering, a person brings the animal again to the priest who kills it and makes an atonement or covering for his sin.

You can see immediately that this can be quite tedious and cumbersome. Besides, the people soon allowed the whole thing to degenerate into a ritual. So that rather than provide them with a point of contact with God, it became an appeasement. What happened is that they would live just the way they liked, but still maintain the sacrifices.

When God saw this, He changed the rules of reconciliation. He now set out to provide the sacrifice by Himself in the death of Jesus Christ. He then ordered that rather than provide mere religion, those who accept that the death of Jesus Christ was their substitute sacrifice for sin, will not only be reconciled to God, but will also have their human spirits quickened so they can begin to live like Adam and Eve his wife did, before they ate the forbidden fruit.

This is what the Bible means where it says:

"For God so loved the world, that he gave his only begotten Son, that whosoever believeth in him should not perish, but have everlasting life." [John 3:16 KJV]

When you answered that 'altar call', what you did was:

- Agree with God that you are a sinner who deserves to die

- Ask for his forgiveness, and seek reconciliation with Him by accepting to quit a life of sin. This is what we call repentance

- Accept that the death of Jesus on the cross of Calvary was your own substitute sacrifice for your many sins

- Accept that because Jesus died in your place, you should now live His life: And the only way to do this effectively is by allowing Him to become your personal Lord and saviour.

That way He can live His life through you.

Repentance

Please tell me more about Repentance

One thing that is helpful when it comes to repentance is to remember that there are 4 parts to it.

Sorrow for sin

One must be sorry for his sins. It is impossible to enjoy sinning and still claim to have repented. The Bible calls it godly sorrow in 2nd Corinthians chapter 7 and verse 10.

Asking the Lord for His mercy and forgiveness.

It is important to remember this because there are some people who do not believe that a person's sins can be forgiven him. They teach that one must pay the full penalty for his sins.Indeed one must pay a full penalty for his sins, that is true. But if someone has paid for you, then you can be forgiven. This is what the psalmist means when he says that the man whose sins are forgiven is truly blessed. This you may find in Psalm 32.

Forgiveness is therefore an act of grace, the grace of God.

Asking God for cleansing in the Blood of Jesus

There are some people who wonder why we should ask for cleansing from all our sins in the blood of Jesus. Some wonder why we should not just simply ask for forgiveness .

The reason lies in what we had shared earlier. The wages of sin is and will always remain death. Therefore each time a person asks to be cleansed in the blood of Jesus, he is meeting the full penalty for sin which the righteousness and the holiness of the Almighty God demands.

Quitting a life of sin

The fourth step is to ask for the help of God not to go back to your sins again. Without this fourth part, repentance cannot be complete. This is because the forgiveness that God provides through the sacrificial death of Jesus is not meant to provide men with a licence to sin. It is meant to provide a gateway to escape from the bondage of sin. You may notice that the Apostle Paul speaking by the Holy Spirit was concerned about this, in his letter to the Romans chapter 6, verse 1, where he asked: "Are we to remain in sin in order that God's grace (favour and mercy) may multiply and overflow? Certainly not! How can we who died to sin live in it any longer?" [Amp. Bible]

Grace

I do hear a great deal about grace

Yes, because grace is at the centre of what God has provided for man through Christ Jesus. It actually means unmerited favour. There is a passage in the Bible that helps us to appreciate this very well.

"For scarcely for a righteous man will one die; yet perhaps for a good man someone would even dare to die. But God demonstrates His own love towards us, in that while we were still sinners, Christ died for us." [Romans 5:7,8 NKJ]

There is also another passage that is quite helpful.

"For it is by grace that you have been saved, through faith - and this is not from yourselves, it is the gift of God not by works, so that no one can boast." [Ephesians 2:8,9 NIV]

An appreciation of the depth of God's grace in Christ Jesus, does create in us a deep sense of gratitude and commitment to Him. This is what Jesus meant when he said that the individual who has been forgiven much, loves much. [Luke 7:47]

27

I believe the apostle Paul was speaking for all of us when he said in Romans chapter 7 from verse 18:

> "For I know that in me (that is, in my flesh) nothing good dwells; for to will is present with me, but how to perform what is good I do not find. For the good that I will to do, I do not do; but the evil I will not to do, that I practice." [Romans 7:18,19 NKJ]

Anybody who has tried making a new year resolution can identify with that sort of frustration. But in spite of that kind of repeated failure, God still stepped in to make provision for our salvation. That is what grace is about.

The Lordship of Jesus

> You know, this question of making Jesus Christ the Lord of my life, is a little bit difficult to comprehend. I do not really see Him: I know I can pray, but I am thinking of some practical relevance. There is really no difficulty in accepting that, but I have some difficulty conceptualizing or figuring out how it is supposed to work practically.

I am glad you raised this question because it is really at the very heart of any meaningful christian life. I believe the first thing we need to appreciate is the basis of accepting Jesus Christ as one's personal Lord and Saviour. Why should you for instance accept Jesus as your Lord and Saviour?

Well, I have already done it now, but I used to wonder quite a bit about that. What helped though was accepting for myself that Jesus Christ is indeed the only begotten Son of God like the Bible says He is. It made it easier to accept Him as Saviour in the light of what we have already discussed now. But other than that, I can't really explain it any further.

Well what you have said does form part of the explanation. It follows that if someone died so that you may live, it may not be that difficult to accept that person as Saviour. It is only a matter of gratitude. But in actual fact, by opting volitionally to die on our behalf, Jesus was seeking to multiply Himself in all of us who will come to accept that His death was on our behalf. What is implied is that if He died the death that we should have died, then we are honour bound if not duty bound to try as much as possible to live the life He should have lived. Here is the way the Bible puts it.

> "Since we believe that Christ died for all of us, we should also believe that we have died to the old life we used to live. He died for all so that all who live - having received eternal life from him - might live no longer for themselves to please themselves, but to spend their lives pleasing Christ who died and rose again for them." [2nd Corinthians.5: 14b-15 LB]

Well I suppose that really follows naturally. But this concept of dying in order to multiply oneself sounds quite strange. Human beings by our nature are not accustomed to that kind of thinking. It is too much of a sacrifice to ask of anybody: the ultimate height of self denial.

Well that is quite true. But actually, it is a concept that Jesus taught, borrowing from the process of multiplication in plant biology, or farming or agriculture, if you please. The setting in which He taught that principle is quite interesting to say the least. It was at one of these great feast festivals in Jerusalem, when there usually were a large gathering of visitors to the city. Many of them obviously must have heard quite a great deal about this itinerant evangelist from Nazareth who demonstrated power and authority over every conceivable thing, from diseases, to evil spirits, to winds and waves, even to death. So naturally, a great many of them thought it was worth their while to meet Jesus. The Bible recorded this incident in John chapter twelve.

> "Some Greeks who had come to Jerusalem to attend the Passover paid a visit to Philip, who was from Bethsaida, and said, Sir, we want to meet Jesus. Philip told Andrew about it, and they went together to ask Jesus. Jesus replied that the time had come for Him to return to His glory in heaven, and that 'I must fall and die like a kernel of wheat that falls into the furrows of the earth. Unless I die I will be alone - a single seed. But my death will produce many wheat kernels - a plentiful harvest of new lives'..." [John 12:20-24 LB]

What actually fascinates me about this story is that Jesus had a very clear vision of His earthly mission, and was not prepared to be carried away by the great popularity that attended His work here. It is a level of detachment that is most impressive. I am sure you do appreciate what I mean.

> Oh yes, I certainly do. Not getting swollen headed in the middle of such a great success, is a tremendous accomplishment.

Oh it certainly is. Through this, He actually borrowed from nature, noting that there is life through death. It sounds a strange concept, but none the less true. It is by virtue of the depth and totality of His sacrifice which reflects His love, that His gospel of love and reconciliation with God and man, is still changing lives today almost two thousand years after His departure.

But let us talk a little bit about how one can appreciate the Lordship of Jesus in his or her life. I suppose the idea of a Lord is not altogether a strange one. A cursory glance at the set up in feudal oligarchies will prove quite instructive. But even then it might be difficult for anyone who has lived all his or her life in an open society to really appreciate this in its true depth.

There is a story or in fact two stories in the Bible that help a great deal. I recall once when I recast one of them in a modern setting, some in my audience were not amused.

Which story is that?

It is that one on the triumphal entry of Jesus into Jerusalem, which we celebrate as Palm Sunday.

How did you put it?

Well you know there was this bit about the fellows who owned the donkey or colt that Jesus rode on.

I think I remember that from my Sunday School days.

Ok, let us just look at the account of it in Mark's Gospel.

"As they approached Jerusalem and came to Bethphage and Bethany at the Mount of Olives, Jesus sent two of His disciples, saying to them, Go to the village ahead of you, and just as you enter it, you will find a colt tied there, which no one has ever ridden. Untie it and bring it here. If anyone asks you, 'Why are you doing this?' tell him, The Lord needs it..." [Mark 11:1-3 NIV]

As a story, it makes some interesting reading until you begin to analyze the implications of it. You know the colt was the prized means of transportation then. So a new colt will be something like a brand new car that you have just bought, which you have never even driven. Say you have just bought yourself a brand new Mercedes or Cadillac or BMW or a Rolls Royce. Then comes a total stranger fiddling with the ignition and trying to start up the car. Then you bark out: *"What on earth do you think you are doing?"*

Then they turn around and look up and say to you: "Oh sorry, we didn't know you were around. *The LORD needs this car now.* He said to just tell you that."

Then you turn around and say: "OK. Its OK. You can go ahead."

Well I can tell you for sure, that is a tough one.

It certainly is. But that is what it means to accept Jesus as Lord. If the Lord needs it, then let Him have it. If the Lord says drop it, then you drop it. If He says: "let go", then you let go. Whatever He says is what you do.

The second story is quite similar in a sense. It was this matter about turning water into wine at the marriage feast in Cana in Galilee as recorded in John chapter two. The mother of Jesus had instructed the servants carefully with these words: *"Whatsoever he asks you to do, do it."*

Now you can see that is a tough one too. And by the way, what Jesus asked them to do wouldn't have made much sense to them or to any of us for that matter. The problem was that the wine had run out. Jesus asked the servants to go and start fetching water. Then after they had filled the pots, He then asked them to go ahead and serve the water to the people. I don't know anybody who wouldn't wonder what the gentleman was up to: some form of joke or something.

But the important thing is that *when they obeyed, it worked; it solved the problem.*

My oh my! That too is a tough one. It worked anyway. It didn't make sense to them, but it worked. I need to remember that.

We all do. Sometimes we think we have figured it all out. But then when we ask Him, sometimes He tells us something we think is way out. But then if we obey it, we find it works; and that is the bottom line. I always have to remind myself too.

I think I am beginning to appreciate how this Lordship is supposed to work.

I am glad you are.

Chapter Two

WHAT IS NEXT?

Now that I am born again, what is next? I am not really quite sure.

The need for Change

There is a song that we sing that depicts this change that must come into the life of an individual after he or she has been born again. Here are the words:

Things are different now, something happened to me
When I gave my life to Jesus
Things are different now, something happened to me
When I gave my life to Him.
Things I loved before, are passed away
Things I love far more, have come to stay
Things are different now, something happened to me
When I gave my life to Him. [Author unknown]

This song actually derives from a passage in the Bible which you will find in 2nd Corinthians chapter 5 and verse 17. The Amplified Bible puts it this way:

"Therefore, if anyone is in Christ, he is a new creation; old things have passed away; behold all things have become new."

The implication of this passage is that once a person becomes a born again christian, he or she should be able to see a difference in his or her life. There would be old lifestyles, old habits, old ways and old thought patterns that would be incompatible with their new life, which they would readily exchange for God's new ways of doing things.

The apostle James actually implied in his letter in James chapter 2 and from verse 14, that if this change or result of the new found faith cannot be seen in any practical way, then the faith itself does not exist.

How does this change come about?

For this change to be effected our thoughts and thought patterns will require some restructuring or turning around. This is the way the bible puts it.

> "And do not be conformed to this world, but be transformed by the renewing of your mind, that you may prove what is that good and acceptable and perfect will of God."
> [Romans 12:2 NKJ]

The major instrument of change is the word of God, the Bible, which you should study for yourself, have it explained to you by others, discuss your understanding of it in fellowship with others in order to enhance your grasp of what it reveals about God, about man, and about life. This is because;

> "All Scripture is given by inspiration of God, and is profitable for doctrine, for reproof, for correction, for instruction in righteousness, that the man of God may be

complete, thoroughly equipped for every good work." [2Nd Timothy 3: 16,17 NKJ]

I would like you to give some examples

There are some passages that detail some of the fundamental changes that should take place. What I will do is outline a few of them here, and then list a good many others for you to check for yourself.

"I advise you to obey only the Holy Spirit's instructions. He will tell you where to go and what to do, and then you won't always be doing the wrong things your evil nature wants you to.

For we naturally love to do evil things that are just the opposite from the things that the Holy Spirit tells us to do; and the good things we want to do when the Spirit has his way with us are just the opposite of our natural desires. These two forces within us are constantly fighting each other to win control over us, and our wishes are never free from their pressures.

When you are guided by the Holy Spirit you need no longer force yourself to obey Jewish laws.

But when you follow your own wrong inclinations your lives will produce these evil results: impure thoughts, eagerness for lustful pleasure, idolatry, spiritism, (that is encouraging the activity of demons), hatred and fighting, jealousy and anger, constant effort to get the best for yourself, complaints and criticisms, the feeling that everyone else is wrong except those in your own little group, - and there will be wrong doctrine, envy, murder, drunkenness, wild parties, and all that sort of thing. Let me tell you again as I have before, that anyone living that sort of life will not inherit the kingdom of God.

But when the Holy Spirit controls our lives he will produce this kind of fruit in us: love, joy, peace, patience, kindness, goodness, faithfulness, gentleness, and self-control; and here there is no conflict with Jewish laws." [Galatians 5:16-22 LB]

These particular passages I am about to detail here tell of real changes in the life of believers.

"All the Jews and Gentiles who lived in Ephesus heard about this; they were all filled with fear, and the name of the Lord Jesus was given greater honour. Many of the believers came, publicly admitting and revealing what they had done. Many of those who had practised magic brought their books together and burnt them in public. They added up the price of the books, , and the total came to fifty thousand silver coins. In this powerful way the word of the Lord kept spreading and growing stronger." [Acts 19:17-20 GNB]

"Meanwhile, Zacchaeus stood before the Lord and said, Sir, from now on I will give half my wealth to the poor, and if I find I have overcharged anyone on his taxes, I will penalize myself by giving him back four times as much.

Jesus told him, This shows that salvation has come to this home today. This man was one of the lost sons of Abraham, and I, the Messiah, have come to search for and save such souls as his." [Luke 19:8-10 LB]

You may check the following references yourself:

ROMANS 1:22-32;   ROMANS 6:1-14;
1ST CORINTHIANS 5:1-13; 1ST CORINTHIANS 6:1-20;
EPHESIANS 4:17 - 32   EPHESIANS 5: 1 - 21
COLOSSIANS 3:1 - 17

All these references speak about the new man or rather the new individual that should emerge after a new birth experience. Some of them speak clearly about the manifestations of the old nature that must be done away with.

When you look at the examples of change quoted above; that is the brethren at Ephesus, and Zacchaeus, you will immediately notice that there was an effort on their parts to live lives that reflect their conversion to Christ. The brethren at Ephesus had among them believers that still practised magic, or consulted mediums. There is still quite a lot of this today among church going people who claim to have believed in Jesus as saviour. But once these people were touched by the power of God, *they made a clean break with such practices.* In my experience, people have brought their charms and meditation books to be burnt. These are signs of genuine conversion.

Restitution

Zacchaeus on the other hand, demonstrated what we refer to as *restitution.* This is the act of making reparations, or paying back for things done in the past. Sometimes the Spirit of the Lord will insist that we go through with this as proof of our genuine conversion. Because some of these issues may prove embarrassing to admit, some people have tended to say that once a person has repented, there was no need for restitution since the Lord has completely forgiven him or her.

There is no doubt that the Lord has fully forgiven, once an individual has genuinely repented, but sometimes, and I do mean sometimes, He may still want us to go ahead and make restitution. He will always urge it on us by stirring our spirit to it. And if the Lord is doing this, then it is not helpful to ignore it as it will imply disobedience to what you are convinced the Lord desires of you. I must hasten to add that restitution usually leads to inner healing of hurts in us and others, particularly when the Spirit of the Lord is urging us to do it.

I once read of a man who used to drop garbage in front of neighbours' doors early in the morning before they woke up. He always enjoyed watching them fume and rage. Then he got converted, and the Spirit of the Lord insisted that he go round and apologise. He was afraid of seeing the rage he had enjoyed at a distance now descend on him. But because he was convinced it was of the Lord, he asked Him for strength, and was able to do it.

That is a tough one indeed. But why do you say sometimes and not always?

I do not think it is helpful to be legalistic about this, since the Lord knows where it will help, and where it may hinder. That is why I prefer to ask the Holy Spirit to direct in this always. Sometimes, the

Lord may say that restitution is required, but that the time is not yet. This is quite important. If you do it when God urges it, it will always help, one way or the other.

I think I understand what you mean.

One thing we must strive against though, is hypocrisy as detailed below. This will lead to self-condemnation if we do not rigorously pursue a genuine change in our lives. We may even end up bringing shame to the name of Jesus as the passage here describes. The moment people know us as born-again christians, then they would have certain expectations of us.

> "You, therefore who teach another, do you not teach yourself? You who preach that a man should not steal, do you steal? You who say, do not commit adultery, do you commit adultery? You who abhor idols, do you rob temples? You who make your boast in the law, do you dishonour God through breaking the law? For the name of God is blasphemed among the Gentiles because of you, as it is written." [Romans 2:17-24 NKJ]

We do have a great responsibility to God and to the body of believers to submit to the Holy Spirit of God to effect these changes in us wherever we need them.

There is something else you may need to bear in mind.

Attitude of old friends

What is it?

Your friends may not approve of your new found life in Christ.

Don't I know that already?

Here is the way the Bible puts it:

"Since Christ suffered and underwent pain, you must have the same attitude he did; you must be ready to suffer, too. For remember, when your body suffers, sin loses its power, and you won't be spending the rest of your life chasing after evil desires, but will be anxious to do the will of God. You have had enough in the past of the evil things the godless enjoy - sex, sin, lust, getting drunk, wild parties, drinking bouts, and the worship of idols, and other terrible sins. *of course your former friends will be very surprised when you don't join them anymore in the wicked things they do, and they will laugh at you in contempt and scorn.* But just remember that they must face the judge of all, living and dead; they will be punished for the way they have lived". [1St Peter 4:1-5 LB]

Habits

What about habits?

I am glad that you raised this question now, because it will enable us to deal with a fundamental principle relating to the walk of an individual before his God. There are some value judgements in life that the individual christian must make under the direction of the Holy Spirit of God that now dwells within him or her. I touched a little bit on this earlier when I was talking about restitution.

When God promised to make a new covenant with man, part of that promise envisaged the capacity of every child of God to tap from the resources of the indwelling Holy Spirit, and the word of God dwelling in their hearts. Here is the way the prophet Jeremiah put it:

> "This is the covenant that I will make with the house of Israel *(representing the new Israel both Jews and non-Jews who are children of faith, who are thus children of Abraham* [Gal.3: 6-9]) after that time, declares the LORD, I will put my law in their minds and write it on their hearts, I will be their God, and they will be my people. No longer will a man teach his neighbour, or a man his brother, saying, Know the LORD, because they will all know me, from the least of them to the greatest, declares the LORD. For I will forgive their wickedness and will remember their sins no more." [Jeremiah 31:33-34 NIV]

The new covenant of grace in Christ Jesus provides for the daily guidance of the Holy Spirit in the life of the individual particularly in areas like this. This is why the Bible declares in Romans chapter 8, verse 14 that " ...*as many as are led by the Spirit of God, are the sons of God." We shall look at this in closer detail later.*

But there is a Bible passage that adequately provides a guiding principle. Here is what it says:

> "All things are lawful unto me, but all things are not expedient: all things are lawful for me, but I will not be brought under the power of any." [1st Corinthians 6:12 NKJ]

This is the way it is rendered in more modern translations:

> "Everything is permissible for me - but not everything is beneficial. Everything is permissible for me - but I will not be mastered by anything." [NIV]

> "I can do anything I want to if Christ has not said no, but some of these things aren't good for me. Even if I am allowed to do them, I'll refuse to if I think they might get such a grip on me that I can't easily stop when I want to." [LB]

The whole point about habits is that many of them affect us in such a way that our resolve or will is weakened. This damage may prove so severe that it actually enslaves us, making us do so many things we would not have done otherwise.

Take alcohol for instance, it has a disinhibiting effect; that is it loosens people up and lowers their moral and spiritual resolve. The same goes for any and every drug of habituation or habit forming drug. They create a kind of dependence that is false, and they undoubtedly do becloud thinking and judgement at high blood levels. King Solomon who drank quite a bit indeed, had these to say:

44

> "It is not for kings O Lemuel - not for kings to drink wine, Nor for princes intoxicating drink; Lest they drink and forget the law, and pervert the justice of all the afflicted. Give strong drink to him who is perishing and wine to those who are bitter of heart." [Proverbs 31: 4-6 NIV]

> "Wine is a mocker, Intoxicating drink arouses brawling, And whoever is led astray by it is not wise." [Proverbs 20:1 NIV]

> "Who has woe? Who has sorrow? Who has strife? Who has complaints? Who has needless bruises? Who has bloodshot eyes? Those who linger over wine, who go to sample bowls of mixed wine. Do not gaze at wine when it is red, when it sparkles in the cup, when it goes down smoothly! In the end it bites like a snake and poisons like a viper. Your eyes will see strange sights and your mind imagine confusing things." [Proverbs 23:29-33 NIV]

There are those who argue that Paul admonished Timothy not to take water only but to use a little wine for his stomach's sake. As a physician by profession I think I can identify with that in the sense that it may have been some commonplace prescription for such indigestion, just like someone would recommend antacids today.

There are those who describe themselves as social drinkers who feel that they do not really have a habit to talk about since they do not really indulge.

There is a passage that the Lord has used to keep many believers safely away from the bottle. Here is what it says:

> "And be not drunk with wine wherein is excess; but be filled with the Spirit." [Ephesians 5:18 KJV]

Whereas they recognize that what is in question here is excess drinking, they also have not failed to notice that alcohol and spirituality seem to be at opposite poles. In other words, the less you have of alcohol, the easier it is for you to discern the Holy Spirit and His moves in your life.

It is interesting to note that the Nazarites in the old testament, who were close to God, were not allowed to touch any alcohol by law.

You may notice that I have discussed this question rather openly. This is as it should be. You may take time to search the scriptures in more detail on this question of habits and ask the Holy Spirit to help you make up your mind.

However if you know that you already do have a serious problem with any of these habits, such an exercise would only serve to continue to have you enslaved by it. The best thing is to ask the LORD to give you the power to break loose in the mighty name of Jesus.

It is also important to note that for some people the whole thing has ceased to be a simple habit. A spiritual force is now using alcohol or the like drug to destroy their lives. If that is your experience, then you will need to be delivered from that bondage.

You can see that given all these potentials for evil, most christians prefer to stay well away from the bottle, and the like habit forming drugs.

But some habits are not mentioned in the Bible. You are quite correct there. The Bible however has general principles to guide a christian who is sincerely in doubt, to determine what the mind of God is in every situation. It is always good to remember that the christian perspective to life in general is often not well appreciated until one is born again. The bible said as much in 1st Corinthians chapter 2 , verses 14 to 16.

"But the man who isn't a Christian can't understand and can't accept these thoughts from God, which the Holy Spirit teaches us. They sound foolish to him, because only those who have the Holy Spirit within them can understand what the Holy Spirit means. Others just can't take it in. But the spiritual man has insight into everything, and that bothers and baffles the man of the world, who can't understand him at all. How could he? For certainly he has never been one to know the Lord's thoughts, or to discuss them with him, or to move the hands of God by prayer. But, strange as it seems, we Christians actually do have within us a portion of the very thoughts and mind of Christ." [LB]

I am sure you can appreciate the above passage. I certainly can. Before I became born again myself, I thought a lot of these things were just funny. Now I know better. But let us look at some of these principles in the word of God which help us to make up our minds on these habits.

The temple of the Holy Spirit

Your body is the temple of the Holy Spirit of God and so must be kept pure for the Lord. This is how the Bible puts it.

"Do you not know that you are the temple of God and that the Spirit of God dwells in you? If anyone defiles the temple of God, God will destroy him. For the temple of God is holy, which temple you are. Let no one deceive himself. If anyone of you seems to be wise in this age, let him become a fool that he may become wise. For the wisdom of this world is foolishness with God. For it is written, He catches the wise in their craftiness. and again, The Lord knows the thoughts of the wise that they are futile." [1st Corinthians 3:16-20 NKJ]

God's desire for our health

God's desire for us is to be in health not for us to deliberately take those things we know are injurious to our health. The Bible puts it this way.

"Beloved, I pray that you may prosper in all things *and be in health*, just as your soul prospers." [3rd John vs.2 NKJ]

Strength in the inner man

It is the will of God that we have strength in the inner man. This is the strength we need to resolve all these conflicts so that we may make spiritual progress heavenward. This inner resolve is so essential for doing the will of God that we should welcome every opportunity to develop it. The Bible puts it this way.

"For this reason I bow my knees to the Father of our Lord Jesus Christ from whom the whole family in heaven and earth is named that He would grant you according to the riches of His glory, to be strengthened *with might through his spirit in the inner man.*" [Ephesians 3:14-16 NKJ]

One may go on and lay many more principles, but I suppose that these ones are enough. They are sufficient to guide us through a number of indulgences, whether they be with food or drinks, or stimulant bearing drugs like tobacco or cigarettes and other such issues.

One thing I find very useful which you may find useful too, is to be downright honest before the Lord. There is one thing I know that deters spiritual progress; and that is *arguing with the voice of the Spirit of God in your life.* If God says quit, there is no need looking for somebody to tell you, "well it does not really matter that much. The issue is not that fundamental." Indeed it may not be, but the Spirit of the Lord within you has said to you: *'QUIT!'* You had better.The gain will always be yours.

Daily Bible Study

I would like to have a good knowledge of the Bible too.

You certainly can. It is not unusual for one to wonder whether he or she can ever have such a working grasp of God's word. I felt the same way soon

49

after I gave my life to Christ. A professor of pathology, a very brilliant one for that matter once said to me: I can't quote the bible the way you do. I simply told him that it was a matter of time and diligent study.

There is one thing that helps an individual develop an aggressively healthy Bible study habit. It is often called, *The Berean Christians' approach to Christian Growth:*

"And the brethren immediately sent away Paul and Silas by night unto Be-re-a: who coming thither went into the synagogue of the Jews. These were more noble than those in Thess-a-lo-ni-ca, in that they received the word with all readiness of mind, *and searched the scriptures daily,* whether those things were so." [Acts 17:10,11 KJV]

A person who has just been born again and is attending a fellowship or church regularly, is hearing a lot and learning a lot rather rapidly. *He or she needs to take time daily to check the Scriptures,* so that the truth he or she is learning day by day will become clearer.

One way to do this is to develop a habit generally referred to as QUIET TIME. This is a time one has set aside to study the Bible and to pray everyday. This is often better early in the morning before one starts the day. Initially one may set aside half- an -hour to study and meditate on God's word, and to pray.

A Bible reading guide is usually quite useful at this stage. Although it breaks up the passages into small portions, it assists the individual to learn a little truth at a time.

Later on, one may need to get Bible study Bibles with cross-references, as well as a study Concordance that will help locate Bible verses. There are also more detailed Bible study courses that are quite useful. Any Christian bookshop will help with details.

These days there are several ways for an individual to gain a quick grasp of the word of God. I have found Bible records or cassettes very useful for gaining an overview of the Bible. An overview creates familiarity with several passages of the Bible and so makes in-depth study much easier particularly with respect to cross-references.

Are there some other tips that may be useful?

Well, it took me quite sometime to realize that the Bible is really a revelation of God to man. And that beginning from Genesis, all the way to the book of Revelation, the task before the individual is to discover God, His ways, His likes and dislikes, and how He has made it possible for us as individuals to get to know Him personally. In the process, we get to learn a lot about ourselves, how God sees us, and how God expects us to see ourselves and our fellow men.

After I came to this realization, it gave my Bible study a very useful orientation. The stories that I read whether in the old or new testaments reveal something about God. So I must not take the stories in isolation, I must look for what they reveal about God. This sort of background is really panoramic and helps to put things in their proper perspective. You may find it useful.

Daily Prayers

Now that you have mentioned quiet time, I might as well tell you that I do not know how to pray.

I have heard quite a number of people say that. From all my discussions with them, I have come to realize what the problem truly is. A good many of these people have come to believe that effective prayer must be said in a certain way. This is not true. Remember that when one is born again, he or she has entered into a father-son, or daughter relationship with God.

When children talk to their parents, they are supposed to talk respectfully, and they usually should feel free to speak out their minds particularly where a good, warm and affectionate family relationship exists.

When people go to God and repeatedly try to say some special words in a special way they have been taught, they create the impression that they are under the stranglehold of religion. The reason is that what they are saying may bear no relationship to the pressures they are facing, which is weighing heavily on their minds. Let us take a simple example.

A factory is having a downturn in its finances. Management has decided that the best way to solve the problem is to prune the staff strength down by retrenching some of the workers. Nobody knows who and who will be affected. There is so much uncertainty. If only new orders would come in, the management may re-consider the retrenchment option.

A Christian member of staff is among those facing the retrenchment option. He goes home to his family with this news, and together they search out an 'appropriate prayer', and begin to recite it until they are weary and all fall asleep. That is what I choose to call the *religious approach*. and this appropriate prayer may be repeated everyday for as long as the situation persists. God is usually not expected to say anything. You will need a special visioner to get that from Him.

As a result of this, many run off in search of diviners and astrologers to assist with the prediction of the future. This is why some who call themselves by the name of Christ patronize these kind of sources in total neglect of the injunction of the Lord in the Bible which says:

"There shall not be found among you anyone who makes his son or his daughter pass through the fire, or one who practices witchcraft, or a soothsayer, or one who interprets omens, or a sorcerer, or one who conjures spells, or a medium, or a spiritist or one who calls up the dead. For

all who do these things are an abomination to the Lord..."
[Deuteronomy 18 : 10 - 12 NKJ]

A Christian who has learnt to converse with God, may find a quiet corner somewhere and discuss the matter as between a father and his son or daughter.

'Dear Lord, what do you think about the problem we have in the office? I am in danger of retrenchment in these very difficult times.

Please Lord, You have to come to our aid. The situation is bad enough as it is, and this may prove the very last straw for many of us.

Dear Lord, are there spiritual forces at work in our factory that may be responsible for this turn of events, or is this a simple case of poor judgement and poor management? Please speak to me Lord, I need to know what is going on. Naturally You can see I am concerned, but I want to tell You that I am confident that You will take care of me no matter what happens. I have committed my life and future into Your hands, and I am quite content to leave them there.'

This type of dialogue prayer will sooner than later elicit a response from the Lord which the individual can appreciate, as the Spirit of the Lord ministers to his or her heart. The Spirit of God will convey the mind of God about the situation to the individual. Once a person can hear God on a particular issue, then whatever the Lord says, is what will be. This is because whatever the Lord says is *truth par excel-*

lence, that is that situation as it actually is or is soon to be.

Well you make it sound very simple. I am sure it is not that simple.

I think the simplest way to put it is that anybody who can talk can pray. I once read about a man who went to God to complain about some members of his church. He wanted the Lord to change them and make them more like Christ or words to that effect. The Lord told him he was the one who needed the change. His only problem was that they did not allow him to dominate them or something like that. But this is the sort of x-ray that goes on before the Lord.

Take the above example of the factory worker for instance, it is possible that God may point out to the christian how their union actions have contributed to the situation, and how he had failed in the past to speak up about excesses of the union leaders.The most satisfying thing about going to God with a situation is that you will soon get to find out the true position of things and whether there is any available remedy.

I really wish it were as easy as you make it sound.

There are initial difficulties getting to know whether it is really the Lord who is speaking. But the only way to overcome such a difficulty is by asking Him repeatedly to speak to you.

You can bet I will begin to try this out today.

That would be wonderful indeed. The result will amaze you, and what you will discover is that the more you make an effort to wait to hear from the Lord, the easier and faster the communication channel becomes, and the richer your testimony of the reality of God in your life.

Chapter Three

I AM WORRIED ABOUT DOCTRINES

This is not an unusual thing in the experience of a young convert. Dispensing with ritualistic religion is often a very difficult thing, and one has a great deal of social pressures added to this.

However, one thing I found very useful is when I was able to make the decision that runs somewhat like this: *The Bible is my final authority in all matters relating to Christian doctrine and conduct.*

After I made this decision, I began to examine my beliefs in the light of God's word. I discovered a great deal of new things that I did not know about. I also discovered a great deal of my religious practices that were indefensible from the point of view of Scripture.

Much later on I was able to determine those that had spiritual significance which had to be done away with, and those that were neither here nor there. This will vary depending on your pre-born again background. But every practice should be judged by scripture. Jesus commanded us to search the scriptures in John chapter 5 and verse 39.

I believe this is a very safe approach particularly because going to God's own heaven where Jesus is, is very serious business. You may need further help in this area and you should consult your base counsellors for more clarification.

There are however some doctrines that the Bible describes as fundamental or foundational. This you may find in Hebrews chapter six, verses one to three.

"Therefore leaving the discussion of the elementary principles of Christ, let us go on to perfection, not laying again the foundation of repentance from dead works and of faith toward God, of the doctrine of baptisms, of laying on of hands, of resurrection of the dead, and of eternal judgement." [Hebrews.6:1-3 NKJ]

Let us look at some of these briefly.

Repentance from dead works

The best way to appreciate this is to look at a few passages that speak directly about it. But before we do that it may be necessary to point out that what is in question here is not works for works sake, but works as a basis for acceptance before the Almighty God. This is why the bible describes it as dead works, because it is incapable of making an individual right before his or her maker.

The works here referred to includes keeping of the laws which will include the ten commandments as well. The whole point here is that nobody has ever, nor can anybody ever keep all the law all the time. So, since one cannot keep all the law all the time, then it is more profitable to come to God *by grace through faith* so that you can always be forgiven and accepted.

"Now we know that whatever the law says, it says to those who are under the law, so that every mouth may be silenced and the whole world held accountable to God. Therefore no-one will be declared righteous in his sight by observing the law; rather through the law we become conscious of sin. But now a righteousness from God, apart from law, has been made known, to which the Law and the Prophets testify. This righteousness from God comes through faith in Jesus Christ to all who believe. There is no difference,for all have sinned and fall short of the glory of God and are justified freely by his grace through the redemption that came by Christ Jesus." [Romans. 3:19-24 NIV]

You may wonder whether this means that christians do not obey the ten commandments. No it doesn't mean that. What it does mean is that by following the Holy Spirit, a christian obeys more than the demands of the ten commandments. This is what Jesus implied in Matthew chapter 5 and verse 20 where He said:

"For I tell you that unless your righteousness surpasses that of the Pharisees and the teachers of the law, you will certainly not enter the kingdom of God." [NIV]

For example, one of the laws in the ten commandments has to do with adultery.

But let us look at what Jesus had to say on this:

"You have heard that it was said, Do not commit adultery. But I tell you that anyone who looks at a woman lustfully has already committed adultery with her in his heart." [Matthew.5:27,28 NIV]

This is the point expressly made by the apostle Paul in his letter to the Romans where he said:

"There is therefore now no condemnation to those who are in Christ Jesus, who do not work according to the flesh, but according to the Spirit. For the law of the Spirit of life in Christ Jesus has made me free from the law of sin and death. For what the law could not do in that it was weak through the flesh, God did by sending His own Son in the likeness of sinful flesh, on account of sin: He condemned sin in the flesh, *that the righteous requirement of the law might be fulfilled in us who do not work according to the flesh but according to the Spirit.*" [Romans 8:1-4 NKJ]

So, the demands of the law including the ten commandments, are more than met in the lives of those who follow the leading of the Spirit of God. And when a person is born again he is supposed to learn to progressively follow the Spirit of God.

Repentance from dead works therefore means, not trusting in anything we are able to do to justify us before God, but rather conscious of the fact that *'all our righteousness are like filthy rags before God'* [ISAIAH 64:6] we should continuously plead the grace of God and the blood of redemption or reconciliation that was shed for us by Jesus Christ.

Faith toward God

Hebrews chapter 11, verse 6 gives us a good picture of what is here implied:

"But without faith it is impossible to please Him, for he who comes to God must believe that He is, and that He is a rewarder of those who diligently seek Him." [NKJ]

The Bible reminds us that;

"No one has seen God at any time..." [John 1:18 NKJ].

Again it tells us that this is because:

"God is a Spirit and they that worship Him must worship Him in Spirit and in truth." [John 4:24 KJV].

It follows therefore that since no one has seen God, the only way to relate and sense God is through the quickened human spirit and so by faith. This is because faith is the only sensor of the spirit. The physical has five senses of touch, sight, hearing, taste, and smell. But *the spiritual has only one sensor, FAITH*. Faith will enable the individual to experience the reality of God in his life and circumstances. Faith is what helps a man to know God. It is faith that produces the experience, which in turn produces the assurance of the reality of God and His interventionist roles in the life and circumstances of the believer. Faith invariably produces the supernatural or the miraculous, which may be so designated either be-

61

cause of its nature or because of its timing. This is why the Bible declares without equivocation that;

"The just shall live by faith." [Romans 1:17]

Again it says;

"He who believes in the Son of God has the witness in himself; he who does not believe God has made Him a liar, because he has not believed the testimony that God has given of His son. And this is the testimony; that God has given us eternal life, and this life is in His Son. He who has the Son has life; he who does not have the Son of God does not have life." [1st John 5:10-12 NKJ]

I will just mention one more of the foundational doctrines in some bit of detail, but will summarize the rest. One gets to learn a lot more with time. Let us talk about the doctrine of Baptisms.

The doctrine of Baptisms

The fact that baptisms rather than baptism was used here, suggests that there must be at least more than one, and indeed there are two cardinal ones, namely: Water Baptism, and Holy Ghost Baptism.

Water Baptism

This follows the experience of the new birth. Where most people usually have some problem is if they had been previously baptized as infants. There are those who argue that God should be able to transfer their infant baptism to count for their post-conversion fulfillment of all righteousness as Jesus called it.

Baptism is symbolic of repentance. The very word means to immerse. So when a person is immersed in water, it signifies his death to sin; when he emerges from the water, it signifies the match to a new life. But Jesus as the perfect man, had no need for baptism, but yet he submitted to it.

> "Then Jesus came from Galilee to John at the Jordan to be baptized by him. And John tried to prevent Him, saying, I have need to be baptized by You, and are You coming to me? But Jesus answered and said to him. Permit it to be so now, for thus it is fitting for us to fulfill all righteousness. Then he allowed Him." [Matthew 3:13-15 NKJ]

When Peter preached his great sermon on the day of pentecost, he urged the people to repent, and be baptized. The implication is that baptism is meant for those who had repented. [Acts 2:38]

Someone may say; 'but this is why we ask them to come for confirmation so that they can re-affirm the faith made on their behalf by their god-parents.' Indeed it may be so for some of the people. But I would prefer to fulfill all righteousness like the Lord Himself did, than stick to tradition. I have always taken the injunction or warning of the apostle Paul in Colossians 2 verse 8 to heart.

> "Beware lest anyone cheat you through philosophy and empty deceit, according to the tradition of men, accord-

ing to the basic principles of the world, and not according to christ." [NKJ]

It might be necessary to find somewhere where believers' baptism is organised and be baptised. I went through believer's baptism at a convention that was inter-denominational. I simply went ahead and fulfilled all righteousness, just like Jesus did.

Holy Ghost Baptism

Since the Bible is the final authority for all doctrine and conduct for the Christian, the best thing is to look at what it has to say.

The disciples were commissioned by our Lord Jesus Christ to go   into all the world and preach the gospel. But they needed Holy Ghost power.

> "Then he opened their minds to understand at last these many Scriptures! And he said, Yes, it was written long ago that the Messiah must suffer and die and rise again from the dead on the third day; and that this message of salvation should be taken from Jerusalem to all the nations: There is forgiveness of sins for all who turn to me. You have seen these prophecies come true.
>
> And now I will send the Holy Spirit upon you, just as my Father promised. Don't begin telling others yet - stay here in the city until the Holy Spirit comes and fills you with power from heaven." [Luke 24:45-49 LB]

Jesus felt his disciples needed the Holy Ghost baptism in order to face the challenges of christian witness in their time. We have another record of it.

"During the forty days after his crucifixion he appeared to the apostles from time to time, actually alive, and proved to them in many ways that it was really he himself they were seeing. And on these occasions he talked to them about the kingdom of God.

In one of these meetings he told them not to leave Jerusalem until the Holy Spirit came upon them in fulfillment of the Father's promise, a matter he had previously discussed with them." [Acts 1:3-4 LB]

"But when the Holy Spirit has come upon you, you will receive power to testify of me with great effect, to the people in Jerusalem, throughout Judea, in Samaria, and to the ends of the earth, about my death and resurrection." [Acts 1:8 LB]

What we can conclude from these passages is that the apostles needed the Holy Ghost baptism to witness for Christ. The question then is, do we in this generation need the same experience? Should we too expect to receive the same experience? Let us see what the apostle Peter said to the crowd on the day of Pentecost, the day he himself received his own Holy Ghost baptism.

"And Peter replied, Each one of you must turn from sin, return to God, and be baptized in the name of Jesus Christ for the forgiveness of your sins; then you also shall receive this gift, the Holy Spirit. For Christ promised him to each one of you who has been called by the Lord our God, and to your children and even to those in distant lands." [Acts 2:38,39 LB]

There are some people who say that the Holy Ghost baptism was only necessary for the early apostles. The fact is that there is nothing we can find in Scripture to justify such a conclusion. Rather what we find is a concerted effort by the early apostles to ensure that anyone who believed in Christ in their time, also received the Holy Ghost Baptism.

"When the apostles back in Jerusalem heard that the people of Samaria had accepted God's message, they sent down Peter and John. As soon as they arrived, they began praying for these new Christians to receive the Holy Spirit, for as yet he has not come upon any of them. For they had only been baptized in the name of the Lord Jesus.

Then Peter and John laid their hands upon these believers, and they received the Holy Spirit." [Acts 8:14-17 LB]

From Paul's encounter with certain disciples in Ephesus in Acts chapter 19, verses 1 to 7, we discern the same trend. He had pointedly asked them: *"Did you receive the Holy Spirit when you believed?"* The implication being that there were people here and there then, who may have believed, but had not received.

Just like there were people in those days who had believed but had not received, so also today. There are lots of people here and there who have believed but have not received.

It therefore behoves all of us who minister, to seek out these ones, and like the early apostles did, help them to receive the Holy Spirit baptism as the apostles received at the very beginning, complete with the accompanying signs of tongues and prophecy.[Acts 10:44-46, and 11:15-17]

I would prefer that we leave off the rest of the foundational doctrines until later. There is always time to catch up on *Laying on of Hands,* the *Resurrection of the Dead,* and *Eternal Judgement.*

Chapter Four

I HAVE SOME OTHER CONCERNS

I would like to know what these fresh concerns are, so we can talk about them too before we end.

I really do thank God very much that He came down and saved me. But I am worried about whether I will be able to stay a born again Christian for a long time. You know, whatever you may say, I know that the Christian life is a big big challenge in a society that is basically corrupt and with several inherent corrupting influences.

There is no doubt about the genuineness of your concerns. Incidentally I had those concerns myself a few months after I was born again. But there are certain things that will help any of us stay on course without consciously making a special effort. I got to learn about some of these after a while and I would share them with you now.

Witnessing

This involves getting others to come and know the Lord Jesus Christ as their personal Lord and Saviour, just like you have done. You may wonder: so soon! Yes indeed, the sooner the better. Look at the way the Bible puts it:

> "For if you tell others with your own mouth that Jesus Christ is your Lord, and believe in your own heart that God has raised Him from the dead, you will be saved. For it is by believing in his heart that a man becomes right with God; and with his mouth he tells others of his faith, confirming his salvation." [Romans. 10:9,10 LB]

Just like this scripture has said, there is nothing that strengthens your faith as much as sharing it with others.

After I gave my life to Christ, I told the immediate members of my family, my brothers and sisters. Then I sat down and wrote to all my friends that I had now become a born again Christian. It really does strengthen your faith a great deal I can tell you.

Besides, there is one other thing it does for you?

What is it?

It puts a kind of check on you immediately if people know that you are now born again. You know, some people may not like that at all.

Yes!

But anyone who is serious about his or her faith, will welcome that. Its like serving notice at home, or at work, that you are now ready to go straight.

People are bound to keep an eye on you and say: "Hey, I thought you were born again? How come you are still into this kind of stuff?" It helps you face the responsibility you now owe to Christ and His body here on earth, to straighten up and shapen up your life in conformity with the word of God. You may not like it initially, but I can tell you, it does help to have people around who can say that to you.

Huh!

I recall my own experience years ago. As an undergraduate medical student, we were just returning from an anatomy dissection class, and a Christian friend of mine was trying to witness.

Then my friends and classmates said something about me that shocked me:

What did they say?

This was the way they put it: "We like Okey's type of Christianity," [meaning myself]; "He does not disturb anybody." You can see that it was indeed a grave indictment. I went home after that, and cried to God to make my faith disturb this "sleep of death" in the lives of my friends and colleagues.

Besides this, there is another very important reason why we should witness. In fact it is the more important reason.

I would like to hear that too.

Jesus commanded us to witness, and He expects us to witness. The way He put it in the Bible, there isn't really much of a choice for anyone who has accepted Him as his or her personal LORD and SAVIOUR.

"And then he told them, *[meaning the believers]*, You are to go into all the world and preach the Good News to everyone, everywhere. Those who believe and are baptized will be saved. But those who refuse to believe will be condemned." [Mark. 16:15,16 LB]

This particular command helps me answer some of my friends and colleagues who claim they were born again too like me, but that the only difference between us is that they did not carry their Bibles about and disturb people like I did. "Christianity," they say, "is a personal thing. You should just keep it to yourself."

Well, I think so too!

But as you can see now, there is no way a born again Christian can hide the Light of God that is shining in him or her. Jesus expects us to put that light on the table so that others can see it and walk by it.

71

This you may check out for yourself in Matthew chapter 5, verses 13 to 16.

Reservations about witnessing

I can see I will have a problem with witnessing. In fact not just a problem, lots of problems.

What sort of problems are these?

The first one is that, I am rather a very shy person. I hardly talk to people about myself. In fact I tend not to talk about myself generally. I really wonder how I can cope with this.

Besides, what will I be saying to them? I hardly know what the whole thing is about myself? You know the way people generally argue about these things. I will just be making a fool of myself.

And I can tell you for sure, nobody will believe me out there. You know, preachers look somehow; forceful, convincing, charismatic: I am not just that way, and I will hate to be rejected.

And what I can't stand is the sneer from all those guys: "even you too." No. It will almost kill me. I used to pity those guys who came around talking about their faith. The guys used to give them a real hard time, and you can bet I did join them some of the time.

Well, that is a whole lot of reservations indeed. One thing I will like to tell you is that if you go out of that door and count one hundred Christians who are witnessing, one hundred of them will tell you that they had some reservations initially, beginning with yours sincerely.

Your very first reservation, *shyness,* was my own first reservation too. I enjoyed my faith, but I had difficulties talking about it. I was to discover later, that I needed to ask for the anointing and quickening of the Holy Spirit.

You will need to explain a little more about that.

There is one man in the Bible whose experience is quite helpful. You remember that when Jesus was about to be crucified, Peter denied three times that he had ever met Him. He couldn't stand up to a young lady to say: "Yes, I know the man; in fact He is my Lord and Master." [Mark 14:66-72]. But on the day of Pentecost and subsequent occasions, he was the chief spokesman of the early disciples. [Acts chapters 1,2,3 and 4]. Let me reproduce a prayer you may find helpful. It was said by the early apostles themselves.

"And now, O Lord, hear their threats, and grant to thy servants great boldness in their preaching, and send your healing power, and may miracles and wonders be done by the name of thy holy servant Jesus." [Acts 4:29,30 LB]

This is how the Lord answered this their prayer.

73

"After this prayer, the building where they were meeting shook and they were all filled with the Holy Spirit and boldly preached God's message." [Acts 4:31 LB]

From all these, you can see that one can begin to ask the Lord for the Spirit of boldness to preach the word of God. Soon you will discover, just like I did, that the whole shyness is gone, and that God has a treasure in you that has been lying idle all these years.

I really do hope and pray so.

Now, let us look at your second reservation; *lack of knowledge of God's word.* This may look such a great handicap initially, but it helps to remember that we are called to be witnesses of what we have seen, heard or experienced. [1st John 1:1-4] If you have ever been to a court, you would have noticed that witnesses are only asked to speak about what they saw or heard. If they are honest witnesses they would not have any difficulties with that, and their story will be consistent each time.

In the Gospel of John chapter 9, verses 1 to 34, the blind man that Jesus healed demonstrated the powers of genuine experience, of an encounter with Jesus. You need to get your Bible and read it. Let me summarize the story.

This gentleman was born blind. Jesus came by him and healed him. When the Jewish leaders heard about it, they called him and asked him. In fact some people wondered if he was indeed the same person. He left them in no doubt. He owned up.

When asked how he came to be seeing, he told a simple story. Jesus made a paste of sand, rubbed it on my eyes, asked me to go and wash it out, and when I did, I came back seeing. These are simple facts of his experience.

The leaders did not believe him, so they called his parents to ascertain whether he was indeed the same blind beggar they all knew. His parents confirmed that he was, but that how he came now to be seeing, they could not tell.

Then the leaders raised what appears to be a theological question about Jesus being a sinner. The man replied with commonsense logic, supplied by the Holy Spirit.

"I don't know whether he is good or bad, the man replied, but I know this: I was blind, and now I see!" [John 9:25 LB]

This is often the crux of the message of a witness.

- "I know what I used to be before I met Jesus Christ."

- "I know where, when and how I met Him."

- " I know what has happened to me since I met Him."

" You can come and share this experience with me."

Anybody who has had a genuine conversion experience can always share this kind of testimony. There is not much of theology there. But where theological questions beyond you are raised, you may resort to what I choose to call *invitational witnessing*. Here is an example.

> "The next day Jesus decided to go to Galilee. He found Philip and told him, Come with me. *[You may say that Philip is now converted]* Philip now went off to look for Nathanael and told him, We have found the Messiah! - the very person Moses and the prophets told about! His name is Jesus, the son of Joseph from Nazareth!
>
> Nazareth! exclaimed Nathanael. Can anything good come from there? *[You may call this a theological question]* just come and see for yourself, Philip declared." [JOHN 1:43,45,46LB]

Indeed one may not be able to answer all the vital questions an honest enquirer may ask. But you may lead them to Church, Fellowship or Bible Class where they can get more help.

With time however, you will be able to pick-up fundamental concepts of the faith with which to confront a potential convert to our Lord Jesus Christ. One thing that I have found useful in recent times is to use the Ten Commandments (Exodus 20:1-17) to create a consciousness of sin, and an awareness of the consequences of continuing sinfulness.(Ezekiel 18:4;

Romans 3:20,23 and 6:23, Galatians 3:24) This is particularly useful in a society that has become very permissive, and where value systems have become quite relative.(Proverbs 28:13, 16:25, 29:1) The Holy Ghost often uses this approach to bring about conviction in the heart of the hearer. (Acts 2:37-39) A person under conviction is ready to hear about the grace and the mercy of God in Christ Jesus, (Romans 5:7,8; Ephesians 1:7) which he or she subsequently comes to embrace with joy and gratitude. (Ephesians 2:8 and 9; Isaiah 1:18-20)

Your third reservation is that *your witness may be rejected.* One thing that is helpful in this regard is to bear in mind that *a witness does not convert anybody.* He simply tells his or her story as honestly and as convincingly as he or she can. The rest of *the work of conviction and conversion of the hearers is left to the Holy Spirit.* It is always good to bear this in mind. If the hearer is willing to make a commitment of his or her life to the Lord, then you should seize the opportunity and lead them in the prayer of repentance and surrender of their lives to Christ.

One must never judge the effectiveness of his or her witnessing activities by statistics. The records are kept by God in eternity. Indeed you may never know that what you said so casually found a fertile soil. But eternity will reveal it.

A person who surrenders his life to Christ today may be a by-product of several inputs by different witnesses. The earlier witnesses served to water the soil of their heart for the seed to grow in due season, at the fullness of time. If you open your Bible to 1st Corinthians chapter 3, from verse 5 you will make this same discovery.

"My work was to plant the seed in your hearts, and Apollos' work was to water it, but it was God, not we, who made the garden grow in your hearts.

The person who does the planting or watering isn't very important, but God is important because he is the one who makes things grow.

Apollos and I are working as a team, with the same aim, though each one of us will be rewarded for his own hard work.

We are only God's co-workers." [1st Corinthians 3:6-9 LB]

That is quite revealing indeed, and certainly quite helpful to know.

In the light of this, it is really impossible to say categorically that your witness is being rejected except of course you have a way of looking right into their hearts to see what is happening. It is often quite helpful not to think too much of what people are saying or how they are reacting. Your experience may be able to tell you that a lot of that is mere facade, or bravado, used to hide a deep need. And oftentimes behind all that, the Holy Spirit of God has found some fertile soil to bury your precious seed.

I pray so.

A lot of what I have said above goes for the sneers from your peers. Sometimes behind all that ridicule lies a solemn wish to obtain what you have. But out of pride and peer pressure they join others to ridicule something they sincerely desire. Those who have the courage of their personal convictions will always dare to be different from the crowd.

I certainly do agree with that.

And if you did dare to be different to become born again, then you must believe that your friends one day will too. I am amazed by the number of my school mates who used to sneer and laugh in those days, who now meet me in conventions and say: "Guess what? I too am born again." All I do is jump and shout, Praise the Lord! Only eternity will reveal whether I was one of those who started them on the road to faith in our Lord Jesus Christ.

I hope you have been able to see that you can begin right away to share your faith with others. If you ask the Lord in prayer to bless every word you speak, and let it find a fertile soil in the hearts of your hearers, the results will amaze you. Again if you ask the Lord in prayer to give you the right words, the result will equally be amazing. Matthew chapter 10 and verse 19, speaks of being given the right words at the right time by the Holy Spirit of God.

Role Model

But permit me to share yet another reservation.
One too many if you insist.

You do not need to worry about that. You will soon discover that virtually all of us had all kinds of reservations. That you feel quite free to talk about them , I consider a very good sign that you are willing to address the issue properly.

I feel encouraged by that. I was beginning to wonder.

You don't need to.

O.K. then. What I am wondering really is whether I will not end up becoming like one of the Christians that I know. He is so quiet, so soft spoken, so ascetic. The picture he paints scares me. I cannot even recommend that to myself, not to talk of re-fashioning another person into that kind of mould.

Well what you will discover when you study the lives of the followers of Jesus in the Bible, very closely, is that they were different personalities. There were extroverts like Peter, emotional, effusive and sometimes explosive; there were introverts like John, deep, meditative.There were also sceptics like Thomas, who needed facts to be convinced. The significant thing at the end of the day is that God transformed each person, and used the natural attributes that they had to extend the kingdom of God on earth in the lives of men and women.

A person like Paul you may describe as a "bulldozer"; an action man. "If you believe it, then go ahead and do it; don't hang around and talk about it." If you look at the Book of Acts, you will discover that he was like that before he got converted to Christ. He believed initially that the Christians were wrong, so he made every effort to eliminate them completely. When he got convinced that they were right after all, he reversed gear with the same zeal and energy, and planted the gospel of our Lord Jesus Christ in many parts of Europe and Palestine. Besides he was very intellectual. You could see from the Bible how God used that to provide us with a lot that is useful today.

We may conclude this by saying that God does not want you to be like someone else. He just wants to transform you, and use you, whether you are noisy or quiet, extroverted or introverted, ascetic or otherwise. The Bible urges us in Hebrews chapter 12 and verse 2, to keep our eyes on Jesus. If we find something worth emulating in another brother or sister, the Holy Spirit may use that their exemplary way to encourage something in us. But that person is not our model. We have only one model, and *that model is no other than JESUS himself.*

This approach has practical value. Suppose you have made Mr. A, or Ms. B your model. Suppose for some reason known or unknown, the said model trips and falls temporarily, or God forbid, permanently, the resultant effect of that is that there will be a chain fall-out effect by all those for whom that individual is the model. If you check 2nd Timothy chapter 4 and verse 10, you will find there the sad report of a man who went back from following Jesus. His name was Demas. Suppose he was a model to some young converts; the danger is that they too might have gone back with him. *that is why JESUS must always remain our model and example, just like the Bible says.*

You may be surprised to hear that I had the same problems as a young Christian. I was then in the university as a pre-medical student. The president of the Christian Union Group in the university then, was a man that was very humble, so soft spoken, never upset. Each time I came to fellowship and saw him, I used to really get worried. I knew there was just no way I could be like that. He was my model then.

But then, the Lord knew I had that problem. During one of those Sunday afternoon fellowship meetings, one speaker came and said words to this effect: "God does not want you to be like someone else. He just wants to change you." I was noticeably relieved. So you can see that what I am sharing with you now is not really original.

Loss of old friends

Talking about this staying on course to the end, I am a little bit worried that I am beginning to part ways with some of my very good friends of old, and I am not making new ones that fast.

Well, that is to be expected, I mean parting ways with some of your good old friends. The way to look at it objectively is to think of the basis of some of those relationships. You may discover that a lot of them are things you will rather do without now that you have been born again.

Being born again does not really imply that one must break with old friends. Not necessarily. What tends to happen however is that the moment you start taking definite stands as a Christian, most of your friends will consider you rather boring these days, going on and on about sin, repentance and the need for salvation. Gradually you will progressively drift apart. But that is not to say that you should not make a concerted effort to keep in touch with them. In fact it is quite likely that God will use you to sow precious seed in their hearts.

What you really need to guard against is being dragged back into the old ways through their pressure. This is the sense in which you may say that being born again creates a dividing line. What it does really is to establish godly, and Holy Spirit inspired, Bible based standards for living, which your erstwhile friends may find unacceptable. I am sure you will share this concern of the Apostle Peter in 2nd Peter chapter 2, from verse 19:

> "For a man is a slave to whatever controls him. And when a person has escaped from the wicked ways of the world by learning about our Lord and saviour Jesus Christ, and then gets tangled up with sin and becomes its slave again, he is worse off than he was before. It would be better if he had never known about Christ at all than to learn of him and afterwards turn his back on the holy commandments that were given to him.

> There is an old saying that "A dog comes back to what he has vomited, and a pig is washed only to come back and wallow in the mud again". That is the way it is with those who turn again to their sin." [2nd Peter 2:19-22 LB]

The danger you will face moving around as before with your old friends just as if nothing has happened to you, is the sort of danger that Lot exposed himself to in Sodom while living among the Sodomites.

> "And turning the cities of Sodom and Gomorrah into ashes, condemned them to destruction, making them an example to those who afterward will live ungodly; and delivered righteous Lot, who was oppressed with the filthy conduct of the wicked (for that righteous man, dwelling among them, tormented his righteous soul from day to day by seeing and hearing their lawless deeds)." [2nd Peter 2:6-8 NKJ]

I think you can afford to spare yourself this kind of torment if that is what it means to keep-on with your old friends. God always knows our needs, and I am sure you will soon make new friends that will encourage you in the Lord.

Let us move on to the next thing that will help you stay on course till the end.

Deep Personal Devotion

The other thing that helps a person stay on course without a conscious effort, is if he or she can develop and cherish a deep personal devotion with the Lord. If one can aim at knowing God deeply and personally, understanding His ways, and striving to follow Him each day, staying on course as a Christian will naturally take care of itself.

Some years ago, I was noticeably worried about this. Two things helped to change the situation for me.

Please tell me what they are

One of them was one of our counsellors at the University of Ibadan. An old English gentleman named Pastor S.G. Elton who has gone on to glory now. It was as if God gave him a mirror into our lives. During one of those group counselling sessions he held for young men and women who wanted to go deeper with the Lord, he had said:

"Let me tell you young men and women", he began in his crackling voice. " Whatever your ambition in life may be, you will never be better than God can make you."

At the end of that session, he called on us to dedicate our lives totally to God.

I responded heartily, convinced in my heart that God and I would be partners in my life together, for my greatest conceivable good.

Somehow it helps for young Christians to know, that a deep personal devotion to God can only work to their greatest advantage, contrary to earlier held notions and beliefs.

You will remember that we had talked earlier about the need for developing a *Quiet Time* habit, where we study the Bible and pray.

What we have just said now actually has to do with *the motivation* for this, and *the depth of commitment* we bring into it. These will determine how much progress we make, and how "effortless" the journey will become in time.

Fellowship with other Christians

I believe the person who said that the Christian life may be likened to the experience of mountaineers attempting to scale a peak, hit the nail right on the head when it comes to the need in the life of the Christian, to fellowship with others.

Mountaineers are accustomed to supporting each other. If anyone loses a vital foothold, those who have firmer footings at the time, rally to help him or her up.

There is nothing like a Christian who is an island, isolated and aloof from the rest. It is the strongest recipe for a short-lived Christian life.

What we see in the Bible, which is true to experience universally, is that those who seek out the fellowship of other believers, serve to strengthen the faith of others, and be in turn strengthened by other peoples' faith.

This is the way the apostle Paul put it to the church in Rome:

"For I long to visit you so that I can impart to you the faith that will help your church grow strong in the Lord. Then, too, I need your help, for I want not only to share my faith with you but to be encouraged by yours: Each of us will be a blessing to the other." [Romans 1:11, 12 LB]

Again in his letter to the Hebrews, he also had this to say:

"Let us not neglect our church meetings, as some people do, but encourage and warn each other, especially now that the day of his coming back again is drawing near." [Hebrews 10:25 LB]

He detailed in his letter to the Corinthian church, how a person should attend fellowship or church, and with what expectations.

"Well, dear friends, let's add up what I am saying. When you meet together some will sing, another will teach, or tell some special information God has given him, or speak in tongues, or give the interpretation. But everything that is done must be useful to all, and build them up in the Lord.

No more than two or three may speak in tongues, and only one at a time, and someone must be ready to interpret what they are saying.

But if no one is present who can interpret, they must not speak out loud. They may speak silently to themselves and to God but not publicly.

Two or three may prophesy, one at a time, if they have the gift, while all the others listen. But if, while someone is prophesying, someone else receives a message or an idea from the Lord, the one who is speaking should stop.

In this way all who have the gift of prophecy can speak, one after the other, and everyone will learn and be encouraged and helped.

Remember that a person who has a message from God has the power to stop himself or wait his turn.

God is not one who likes things to be disorderly and upset. He likes harmony, and he finds it in all the other churches." [1st Corinthians 14:26-33 LB]

I am sure you can see from all these, that when a person attends a fellowship of Christians, he or she goes with a view to be blessed, and to be used by the Lord to bless others.

A person may well say: "I don't really think I need any fellowship."

That may well be true. But he or she certainly cannot say that the fellowship does not need him or her. That is left for the fellowship to decide. You may check out 1st Corinthians 12: verses 12 to 27 for more information.Here is what verse 27 says:

"Here is what I am trying to say: {ie. a kind of summary} all of you together are the one body of Christ and each one of you is a separate and necessary part of it." [LB]

Dependence on the Holy Spirit

We have said quite a few things about this before. All that is left here is to highlight a few more practical details.

I have always believed that one should *lean on the Holy Spirit so heavily that He can almost literally feel your weight.* I did not know this at all when I gave my life to Christ. But over the years I have come to realize that following your Spirit guide in every situation everyday, is the surest way to get yourself on the shores of eternity in due course.

When I expressed my own concerns about the future, I recall what the Lord said to me one day at the chapel gardens of the University of Ibadan. He told me that if I can follow Him each day, one day at a time, then I will follow Him till the end. It has stayed with me ever since.

You will notice that this is not new at all. In fact our Lord Jesus Christ repeated it quite often in His popular statement: *'Sufficient unto the day is the evil thereof.'*

Let us end this by saying that our future is secure in the hands of Jesus, provided we are quite willing and quite satisfied to leave it there.

Chapter Five

JUST BEFORE WE PART

I would like to share a few things with you before I leave.

Please go ahead.

The love of God for you

The first one is the Love of God for you

That would be quite interesting. I have wondered about that in the past. I am glad you mentioned it. Please go on.

There is something that is quite helpful to know, no matter what the situation in your life may be at anytime.

And what may that be please?

Its probably better to put it in the form of a maxim: *God loves me no matter what.*

Well! I am sure you will agree that that needs some explanation. It isn't that obvious all the time. Certainly not.

91

I do know what you mean, like in difficult and unpleasant situations and when things really go awry. Yes I do know. In fact it is at such times more than any other that you need to remind yourself, that no matter what is happening in your life and circumstance, you can depend on the love of God to see you through. This attitude is based on a few solid facts about God.

Please go on

- God knows everything that has happened or will happen to you.
- The Love of God will always provide you with a way of escape in every situation.
- God can do whatever He has said in His word anytime and any day.

Now let us look at these a bit more closely. The first one deals with *God's Omniscience.*

You know, that is where I have the problem. If indeed He knows, then why does He let some of these things happen?

Well that is probably too much for anyone to say sometimes, why things happen, except of course they have a revelation from the Lord. But that is not as important as knowing that whatever may happen, you can handle through the Love, Grace, and provisions of Power and authority in Christ Jesus.

This is what turns an adverse situation into a testimony, when it provides us the opportunity to demonstrate the love and the power of God that is at work in us.

This is why it is important that you remember that God always provides a way of escape in every situation however tempting.

"But remember this - the wrong desires that come into your life aren't anything new and different. Many others have faced exactly the same problems before you. And no temptation is irresistible. You can trust God to keep the temptation from becoming so strong that you can't stand up against it, for he has promised this and will do what he says. HE WILL SHOW YOU HOW TO ESCAPE TEMPTATION'S POWER so that you can bear up patiently against it." [1st Corinthians. 10:13 LB]

I believe what the Bible is saying here is that God expects us not to buckle but to use the authority He has provided for us in Christ Jesus to correct the adversities in our circumstances. You should check out these references: EPHESIANS 1:15-23; 3:14-21; PHILIPPIANS 2:5-11; 4:13; COLOSSIANS 2:9,10;

There are quite a number of passages to check out, but may be we should defer that till another visit. You should however note one of the passages listed above:

"Now glory be to God who by his mighty power at work within us is able to do far more than we would ever dare to ask or even dream of - infinitely beyond our highest prayers, desires, thoughts, or hopes." [Ephesians 3:20 LB]

It is comforting to know that the power that God uses to answer prayers and perform miracles beyond our wildest imagination, is already at work within us. It is possible to tap that power and use it for ourselves and others. You can begin to tap it now by learning to use the authority in the NAME and the BLOOD of JESUS.

Temptation

I would like you to talk a little bit more about temptation which you mentioned earlier. Sincerely, I'd rather not have temptation at all, than look for a way of escape.

I suppose what you have said goes for each and everyone of us. The Bible teaches that we can learn to be victorious in temptation and that there is usually a reward at the end.

"Happy is the man who doesn't give in and do wrong when he is tempted, for afterwards he will get as his reward the crown of life that God has promised those who love him.

And remember, when someone wants to do wrong it is never God who is tempting him, for God never wants to do wrong and never tempts anyone else to do it. Temptation is the pull of man's own evil thoughts and wishes.

These evil thoughts lead to evil actions and afterwards to the death penalty from God." [JAMES 1:12-15 LB]

The best time to begin to fight temptation and sin is at the pull stage. Its no use waiting till you are trapped in it before you can begin to look for a way of escape. Once you notice the pull towards evil, begin to rebuke the forces of evil in the mighty name of Jesus. Ask the Lord to show you what to do to escape the pull of that temptation. Once He shows you what to do, then go right ahead and do it in obedience.

This is just a parting shot. You may dismiss it in a few sentences on your way out.

What is it? If it is important to you, I will spare the time.

Going to church

Well, I don't know how you will feel about this, but what do you think about belonging to a church? I haven't been to church in ages, and I think all these churches are the same.

Well I am glad you asked this question. I remember the late Pastor S.G. Elton giving us an old man's wise saying. He said to us: *"If you ever find a perfect church, do not join it. The moment you do, it will cease to be perfect."* No human organisation is perfect, so no one expects the church to be perfect.

But when you know that fellowship is a two way traffic, you join a church where you can be fed, and also help to feed others. A church always provides a useful forum for Christian service, and for Christian growth.

Is there nothing that should guide an individual as to which church to join?

This is the sort of question one must answer with extreme caution, knowing how various denominations protect their membership. But personally what has always guided me is where the word of God is expounded and my soul is nourished. This sort of forum may be found in various denominations. One way I judge the spiritual food I receive anywhere I go, is to ensure that they are based strictly on the word of God and that the teacher is always able to cite his or her authority; book, chapter and verse. The same also goes for forms and rituals.

This is what has been called the Berean Christians' approach which was mentioned earlier - Acts 17:11. They received the word of God, and searched the scriptures daily, whether they could find adequate correlation.

Having said this, one must be careful to avoid so called Christian groups whose rituals smack of spiritism.

Exactly what do you mean by that?

Spiritism involves contact with demon spirits who are under the control of the devil or Lucifer. The best thing to have is an inquiring mind. Ask questions about practices; are they based on scripture? What about the prescriptions for special prayers and the like; is there any biblical basis? If there is a genuine doubt, and you suspect that the practices are not in line with God's word, then the best thing is to opt out and go somewhere else.

A high index of suspicion is often required. Whenever there is so much emphasis on visions and demonstrations of power with little or no concern whatsoever for holiness, I believe one must begin to be suspicious. *The gift of discernment of spirits*, given by the Holy Spirit comes to our aid in this regard. We shall talk about this another time.

One thing the Bible teaches about the servants of God is that they turn men and women to seek the Lord in holiness and righteousness. You can hear our Lord Jesus Christ talk about it in these words:

> "Which of you can truthfully accuse me of one single sin?" [John 8:46 LB]

This was the same point the apostle John was making by the Holy Spirit in his letter.

> "Oh, dear children, don't let anyone deceive you about this: if you are constantly doing what is good, it is because you are good, even as he is.

> But if you keep on sinning, it shows that you belong to Satan, who since he began to sin has kept steadily at it. But the Son of God came to destroy these works of the devil. The person who has been born into God's family

does not make a practice of sinning, because now God's life is in him; so he can't keep on sinning, for this new life has been born into him and controls him - he has been born again. *so now we can tell who is a child of God and who belongs to satan. Whoever is living a life of sin and doesn't love his brother shows that he is not in God's family.*" [1st John 3:7-10 LB]

You may check out 1st John 2: 1 and 2 by yourself.

An adequate fellowship of believers for spiritual growth will be a place where people are not just encouraged to give their lives to Christ and be born again, but also where they are encouraged to pursue holiness with vigour and to develop a deep personal walk with God.

Like I said, this exists in several denominations. God has moved into well established denominations with the message of the new birth as an individual experience, that the gaps are truly beginning to close as the hunger in the hearts of men for God is being met. Some pastors in very well established church groups are now permitting fellowships within their churches that encourage people in this way and many born again Christians are feeling the call of God to stay in their denominations to work so that others may see the Light too.

For a new convert though, the emphasis is on feeding and spiritual growth. Where this is not available where you are, you may find it in a group fellowship that may not necessarily involve changing your denomination. You may then go on to your home base to share the things that you are learning from the word of God if and where they let you.

The other thing that one should look out for are *heresies.* You may say that as a new convert, you would have problems here. That may be true. But Jesus did sound a strong note of warning with these words, in Matthew chapter 24:

> "Take heed that no one deceives you. For many will come in my name saying I am the Christ, and will deceive many. Then many false prophets will rise up and deceive many.
>
> Then if anyone says to you, Look, here is the Christ! or There, *do not believe it.* For false Christs and false prophets will arise and show great signs and wonders, so as to deceive, if possible, even the elect. See I have told you before hand. Therefore if they say to you, *look He is in the desert! do not go out, or look, He is in the inner rooms! do not believe it.* For as the lightening comes from the East and flashes to the West, *so also will the coming of the son of man be."* [Matthew 24:4,5,11, 23-27 NKJ]

As you can see from the above passages, the danger can be averted by a working knowledge of the word of God, the Holy Bible. The fact that Jesus said that even the elect is in danger of being deceived should make us guard our faith jealously against all heresy. *and the only way to judge heresy is to measure it against the revealed word of God in the Bible.* Any doctrine that does not measure up to the truth as stated in the word of God, deserves only to be dumped in the garbage can where it rightly belongs.

But then as a young convert, I am quite vulnerable.

Only to a limited degree. God who has called you out of darkness into His marvelous light, will keep you, [1st Peter 1:5] provided you are determined in your heart to serve Him sincerely. Stories abound of people who were misled for a while. But the love of God found them and opened their eyes to the truth in God's word, and as soon as the truth dawned on them, they changed course. It does not have to be that way. A prayerful watch, ardent study of God's word, and constant fellowship with God's people will help a great deal to protect the individual. Most people go into these errors when they are under pressure, or have isolated themselves from the rest of the brethren. Others as a result of craving for new things. One can always be quite careful and prayerful. A safe rule is never to let yourself go beyond your depth too fast. You need time to consolidate the many new things and principles you are learning about following God. The Bible cautions us with these words in Ephesians 4, verse 14.

> "Then we will no longer be like children, forever changing our minds about what we believe because someone has told us something different, or has cleverly lied to us and made the lie sound like the truth." [LB]

100

Part of what is implied here is that the various gifts that the Lord has given to His church or body of believers, will be used to steer us all away from error. You may check this out from Ephesians 4: 11 - 16. How to recognize these gifts and those who have them are subjects for another day.

This has been a wonderful visit. I have really gained a lot. But nevertheless, I should not let you go without asking this question.

If you insist, why not.

I know you said quite a lot about joining a church. I think I agree with you now that it is something a Christian ought to do as part of his or her effort at spiritual development. But you know I am quite worried about some of the things I hear about these churches, particularly the ones that emphasize that one must be born again.

Exactly what are you worried about?

Well it is this question of asking people to bring ten percent of their earnings. I doubt that they have any authority in the Bible to do that. It sounds so unfair to collect so much money from people that way. I doubt that I will stay in any church where they teach that.

Well, believe you me I am quite happy that you mentioned this. You may be surprised to hear that I felt the same way too after I gave my life to Christ. Mine was actually for a different reason. I felt that removing ten percent from what I had would create more problems for me. I was an undergraduate in the university then. I really felt that I couldn't part with that much.

So what made you change your mind?

Well, it is a long story, and I am not quite sure you would want to hear it all today.

If you can wait to tell it why not?

Of course I can wait to tell it.

Chapter Six

THE MINIMUM GIFT

Before I resume my personal testimony, I suppose I need to tell you some of the principles that are related to giving of one's substance towards the furtherance of the gospel.

Please go on

One way to look at it, is to try and visualize what it cost Jesus to bring us our redemption. But please don't get me wrong. I am by no means implying that I saw it all so clearly from the beginning. By the time you have heard my own story, you will see why I am careful to mention this, so you do not get discouraged.

Please just go on. I am dying to hear the whole story.

I recall a tract I saw many years ago on this. It was put pictorially, and served to drive the message home. There were ten loaves of bread illustrated. The gentleman kept nine in one heap, and held one grudgingly in his hand. The nine loaves had this written over them: FOR SELF. The one loaf in his hand had: FOR

GOD written on it. And then below the picture was this: Who could be so mean as to give less.

I believe the letter to the Philippian church detailed what it cost our Lord Jesus Christ to bring down our salvation, and through that stated a very very vital principle that may be summarized in these words: *the way up is down.* In other words, the way to material progress and prosperity is not to hold on to what you have, but to give. The more you give, the more you receive, so you can give more. Here is what the Bible says in Philippians chapter two.

> "Your attitude should be the same as that of Christ Jesus: Who being in very nature God, did not consider equality with God something to be grasped but made Himself nothing, taking the very nature of a servant , being made in human likeness. And being found in appearance as a man, he humbled himself and became obedient to death - even death on a cross!" [Philippians 2:5-8 NIV]

You may say that Jesus was on His descent in these verses. He was God, but for our sakes, He abandoned all the privileges of deity to take on the limitations of humanity. Consequent upon that descent, he found that He needed to even go lower, to die the death of a criminal, in order to achieve redemption for us.

This is tremendous sacrifice, and the Bible tells us in the book of Hebrews chapter 12, what inspired it:

> "Let us fix our eyes on Jesus, the author and perfecter of our faith, *who for the joy set before Him,* endured the cross, scorning its shame, and sat down at the right hand

of the throne of God. Consider him who endured such opposition from sinful men, so that you will not grow weary and lose heart." [Hebrews.12:2-3 NIV]

Jesus was very much conscious of the reward of His tremendous sacrifice. We who believe, are that reward. Each day as we experience the victory and power that is ours in Christ Jesus, He is pleased with the fruits of His labour.

Now, If an individual has received this Good News of redemption in Christ, it will be naive to imagine that it does not cost money to disseminate. Printing of tracts, translating and printing Bibles, paying the wages of ministers of God, building sanctuaries and places of worship etc.: All these cost money. Who does God expect to pay these bills but the beneficiaries of the blessing? If the truth in God's word has blessed your life, kept your home, kept you healthy, protected you, prospered your business etc. then paying to disseminate or publicize that truth so that others may benefit should be your joyful responsibility.

Actually the way you have put it now, one wonders if there is any justification not to pay. But then it does not have to be ten percent strictly, does it really? I know some people cannot afford to spare ten percent of their income on a regular basis.

Well now that you have mentioned it, I think it is time for me to continue my story.

Yes.

Well I was actually in need when I stumbled at this truth in God's word several years ago. I needed to assist my family to support my education in the University. I asked the Lord to come to my aid and provide me with some sources of income.

In our university fellowship then, there was a need for money. They were owing some department some money for services rendered to the fellowship. They taught us to give up ten percent of our income and that God will provide for us according to His promised word in Malachi chapter three and verses eight to twelve:

"Will a man rob God? Yet you rob me, But you ask, 'How do we rob you?' In *tithes and offerings*. You are under a curse - the whole nation of you - because you are robbing me.

Bring the whole tithe into the storehouse, that there may be food in my house, Test me in this way says the Lord Almighty, and see if I will not throw open the floodgates of heaven and pour out so much blessing that you will not have room enough for it. I will prevent pests from devouring your crops, and the vines in your fields will not cast their fruit," says the Lord Almighty. Then all the nations will call you blessed, for yours will be a delightful land, says the Lord Almighty." [Malachi 3:8-12 NIV]

The ten percent you are complaining about is really what the Bible calls the *tithe*. But the Bible also talks about offerings. So in fact what we are talking about is not just tithe, but tithes and offerings for the furtherance of the Gospel of Jesus Christ, which has now come to mean so much to us.

After I was told about this, I went to the Lord and promised that if I could earn some new money, then I would start paying from there. I told Him that what I had then was not enough for anything.

You know, God said something to me that was quite interesting.

When you say God spoke to you, what exactly do you mean?

Well, He spoke to my heart; it was not an audible voice. But I knew in my heart it was God. You get to learn sooner or later how God speaks to you. You see, what you have come into is a relationship, and relationships by nature are two-ways. You speak to God, and God talks back to you. But may be we should leave that for another time.

O.K. What exactly did He say?

He told me that if I couldn't pay from what I had, there was no guarantee that I would pay from what I get.

And what did you say to that? Because I think that is true.

Well, I asked the Lord to trust me. That I certainly would pay from the new one. The one at hand was just not enough.

He wouldn't say anything after that, and my situation rather than improving actually deteriorated. Things actually got worse for me. And if you look at that passage we have just read, you will notice that it says something about preventing pests from eating away what you have.

Anyway, to cut a long story short, I decided to pay when things were not getting any better. After I gave my tithe, I became like a bird let out of a cage. I spent the rest of my little money buying books and Bible study guides for my students in the Scripture Union groups that I visited. We were called senior friends in those days by these students. Two to three weeks after this, all my money had gone. I remember that day clearly as if it was yesterday.

What did you do? It must have been a desperate moment.

You bet it was. I recall that I knelt by my bedside that morning and said a prayer that is somewhat like this: "LORD if this thing is working, then it had better work now. You can see that my money is completely finished". It wasn't a long prayer at all.

And what happened?

It was like fiction, almost incredible. Long before that I had written a play for radio. I had been to the station several times, but the producer kept telling me that he had not had time to look at my work. So after numerous fruitless trips that drained whatever little money I had, I gave up.

But that morning when I got to the lecture theatre, that producer was there by our anatomy lecture theatre. He was not looking for me. He had come to see someone else. But then he saw me and called me, and told me that he had actually used one of my plays, and that I had six pounds and six shillings to collect. You could have knocked me down with a feather.

I bet one could have indeed. This is interesting, very interesting indeed.

You will now understand why I believe rather very strongly that *giving your money or time or talent to support the work of the gospel is actually doing yourself a favour.* Because if you give cheerfully with the understanding and burden that someone else should hear this gospel that has done so much good in your life, then God will ensure that you have enough and to spare so you can continue to give. This is the way the Bible actually puts it.

"Remember this: Whoever sows sparingly will also reap sparingly, and whoever sows generously will also reap generously.

Each man should give what he has decided in his heart to give, not reluctantly or under compulsion, for God loves a cheerful giver. And God is able to make all grace abound to you, so that in all things at all times, having all that you need, you will abound in every good work.

Now he who supplies seed to the sower and bread for food will also supply and increase your store of seed and will enlarge the harvest of your righteousness.

You will be made rich in every way so that you can be generous on every occasion, and through us your generosity will result in thanksgiving to God.

This service you perform is not only supplying the needs of God's people but is also overflowing in many expressions of thanks to God.

Because of the service by which you have proved yourselves, men will praise God for the obedience that accompanies your confession of the gospel of Christ, and for your generosity in sharing with them and with everyone else.

And in their prayers for you their hearts will go out to you, because of the surpassing grace God has given you." [2nd Corinthians. 9:6-8, 10-14 NIV]

Well, I have always believed in contributing my widow's mite in those days.

I hope you recognize what that really means.

Well it means the little you can afford.

No, not really, that is not what it means. I think we had better look at the passage and see exactly what it says:

> "Jesus sat down opposite the place where the offerings were put and watched the crowd putting their money into the temple treasury. Many rich people threw in large amounts But a poor widow came in and put in two very small copper coins, worth only a fraction of a penny. Calling his disciples to him, Jesus said, "I tell you the truth, this poor widow has put more into the treasury than all the others.
>
> They all gave out of their wealth; but she, out of her poverty, *put in everything - all she had to live on.* " [Mark 12:41-44 NIV]

So you can see that the widow's mite isn't giving the tithe, or ten percent, but one hundred percent. It took me quite sometime to realize this. I used to think like you that the widow's mite meant the little you can afford. It means all that you have in your storehouse or bank account. May be you need to think twice about the widow's mite after today.

Well I can tell you it will not be easy.

Nobody says it is easy to start with. But after you have started I am sure you will be able to say like David in Psalm 34 verse 8: "Oh taste and see that the Lord is good. Blessed is the man that trusteth in Him."

111

You know, part of the problem I will have is the lifestyle of some of these preachers. That will worry me.

Why should that worry you? Is it because they are preachers?

Not really, but I think they should live moderately to encourage those who give. You don't want to feel that all you are doing is making them live in luxury.

Well, I think the best way to look at this, is to *know who you are giving your money to.* When you sow a seed for the furtherance of the gospel, you are not really giving the money to the preacher, *you are giving it to God.* God will bless and prosper you for giving to Him and to His work. If the preacher happens to misuse it, he or she will answer for that before the Lord. As you read the Bible later on you will find that all these things are well taken care of. I will just give you a few examples.

In the old testament of the Bible, you will find that God made very adequate provision for the ministers of the law to be well fed and well taken care of. You may check these out in Leviticus Chapters 2, verses 1 to 3, and verse 10; and 10, verses 12 to 15, as well as Malachi chapter 3, verses 8 to 12.

But there were those who abused it, and if you check the records, you will see that God punished them for it. One example is the sons of Eli in 1st Samuel chapter 2, verses 12 to 17. In fact you need to see what verse 17 says:

"This sin of the young men was very great in the Lord's sight, for they were treating the Lord's offering with contempt."

You may check out the rest of that judgement in 1st Samuel chapter three, verses eleven to fourteen.

Well I hope some of these guys have seen these scriptures you are quoting.

Well it is not really our place to stand in judgement of anyone. God is the judge of us all. I always try to remember that. It was David who said: If you regard iniquity Oh God, who will stand. But that is not to say that ministers as custodians of the offering of God's people to the Lord, towards the extension of His kingdom, do not have a responsibility to walk in integrity. They do, and this is the way the apostle Paul put it:

"I am sending another well known brother with him, [ie. referring to Titus] who is highly praised as a preacher of the Good News in all the churches. In fact, this man was elected by the churches to travel with me to take the gift [ie. referring to their offering] to Jerusalem. This will glorify the Lord and show our eagerness to help each other. *by travelling together we will guard against any suspicion,* for we are anxious *that no one should find fault with the way we are handling this large gift.* God knows we are honest, *but I want everyone else to know it too.*

That is why we have made this arrangement.[2nd Corinthians 8:18-21 LB]

I have no doubt in my mind that most ministers of the Full Gospel of our Lord Jesus Christ are quite conscious of the great responsibility they owe the body of Christ to walk in conscience and integrity before the Lord in every area. This is the way the apostle Paul put it.

"We try to live in such a way that no one will ever be offended or kept back from finding the Lord by the way we act, so that no one can find fault with us and blame it on the Lord. In fact, in everything we do, we try to show that we are true ministers of God." [2nd Corinthians 6:3 - 4 LB]

Well, well, well. I suppose I am convinced really. I pray that God will help me to start this immediately. But tell me how will He return what I have given?

I doubt that anyone can say that with any precision. But that He will return it, is something even I can guarantee on His behalf, after over eighteen years of walking in this way. He always returns in abundance, much greater than you gave. This is the way the Bible puts it:

"Give, and it shall be given unto you; good measure, pressed down, and shaken together, and running over, shall men give into your bosom. For with the same measure that you mete withal it shall be measured to you again" [Luke 6:38 KJV]

I had an occasion to learn what the Bible meant here by: "shall men give into your bosom" firsthand.

What happened?

I had just bought a new car and wanted to take out a comprehensive insurance on it. My insurance agent told me that I had lost my No Claims Bonus, which was to have reduced my premium by 50%. I got to church the next sunday, and the Lord asked me to give a certain offering. I did. When I went to my agent subsequently, hoping to pay another installment towards my premium, I was pleasantly surprised to hear that my bonus had been re-instated, and that what I had paid so far had actually covered my premium. So really, no one can say how God will return a gift by a cheerful giver. *But what I can say for sure is that He always does.*

Well this has been wonderful, quite an eye opener. I have enjoyed it.

I am glad you have.

But let me say this in addition. After you have started giving towards the extension of the kingdom of Jesus here on earth, you will discover that tithing as good as it is, is simply a kind of school master, to train us to learn to give. The idea behind the giving of the widow we have just talked about, is in fact more consistent with the new testament teaching on giving.

I hope you are not implying that we should give all we have away?

Not really. But the principle is that Christ was willing to give all He had away for us. In His own case, it happened that God demanded it of Him, so He had to give it. The example He has laid for us is that we too must learn to be willing to give all that we have away for the extension of the kingdom for which Jesus came and died. Once we are willing, then whatever fraction of it that God demands of us, I say God, not the preacher, we shall give. This is why the apostle Paul admonished that everyone should give as he or she has purposed in his or her heart. What that means in essence is giving as the Holy Spirit of God has directed no matter how persuasive or unpersuasive the preacher may be.

I can see that we need to take time to discuss how one can actually hear from God then. That will assist us to give what God wants us to give, when He wants us to give it, and where He wants us to give it for the extension of the kingdom of God in the heart of men and women.

You are certainly right there. God will then be able through us all, to distribute the resources available, to areas where there are needs, in order to avoid waste in the world wide family of God.

That will be something like Divine Economic Planning.

More like Divine Budgeting if you please.

Yes

I can bet you we are still quite far from there.

Not really. As more and more individuals learn to hear from and obey the voice of the Holy Spirit in their lives, then like a jig-saw, assembled piece by piece, the whole will gradually emerge.

We all pray so.

Chapter Seven

THE ASSURANCE OF SALVATION

But just before I leave, I would like to ask you my own parting question.

What is the question?

You may pardon my asking it: but are you truly born again?

I certainly am, and I mean every word of it.

What makes you so certain about that?

Well, I don't really know for sure, but I know I am born again. I feel it within me, and have felt it ever since that very day that I gave my life to Jesus Christ. In fact it has been most exciting I can tell you.

What times do you feel it most?

Oh times like these, when I am meditating on the word of God and sharing with other people. I feel that assurance within me.

That is very lovely indeed. I am glad that you do feel it. The Bible says in Romans 8:16 that the Spirit of God bears witness with our spirit that we are children of God. That is wonderful indeed. Every child of God does get to feel that he or she is born again sooner or later.

But you know, being born again is really not a matter of the way you and I feel. If it were, then it will vanish the day we do not feel it anymore. It is important to remember that the assurance of your salvation depends entirely on the promise of God. You can depend absolutely on what God has said in His word. This is because GOD DOES NOT CHANGE. He said in Malachi 3:6; *'I am the Lord I change not.'*

If God said that if you surrendered your heart to Jesus you would be born again, then that must settle the matter. It does not matter what I, the devil nor anybody for that matter feel about it. It does not even matter whether you yourself feel saved or not. Like I said, you eventually get to feel saved, and I am glad that you do. But that is like the "icing on the cake". It is not the cake itself. Your salvation is rested firmly on the promise of God in His word that: 'If thou shalt confess with thy mouth the Lord Jesus, and shall believe in thine heart that God raised Him from the dead, thou shalt be saved.' You may check this out again in Roms.10:9 It is always good to remember that, and let the devil know, that you know for sure on what your salvation is based.

119

Well I am glad you mentioned this, because the other day I didn't really feel that saved.

Why?

Well, somebody upset me very badly, and I really "blew my top". After that I didn't feel that saved anymore until this evening when you came, and we started this fellowship.

Well, that is the point I am making. If you do anything wrong after you have been born again, and the Spirit of God within you points it out to you, all you need to do is to genuinely repent, and ask the Lord for His forgiveness. Sometimes, there may be the need to make restitution as the Spirit of the Lord directs as we mentioned earlier. But that has nothing to do with the covenant relationship that you have made with your God in Christ Jesus. This is the way the Bible puts it.

"But if we are living in the light of God's presence, just like Christ does, then we have wonderful fellowship and joy with each other, and the blood of Jesus His Son cleanses us from every sin.

If we say that we have no sin, we are only fooling ourselves, and refusing to accept the truth

But if we confess our sins to Him, He can be depended on to forgive us and cleanse us from every wrong. [And it is perfectly proper for God to do this for us because Christ died to wash away our sins.]

If we claim we have not sinned, we are lying and calling God a liar, for He says we have sinned.

My little children, I am telling you this so that you will stay away from sin. But if you sin, there is Someone to plead for you before the Father. His name is Jesus Christ, the one who is all that is good and who pleases God completely." [1st John 1:7-10, 2:1-2 LB]

A Christian who is born again may be overtaken in a fault like the Bible says in Galatians 6:1. The implication is that he or she has not planned to sin. But was unfortunately scuttled by the devil.

This is what the Bible means where it says:

"The person who has been born into God's family does not make a practice of sinning, because now God's life is in him; so he can't keep on sinning, for this new life has been born into him and controls him - he has been born again." [1st John 3:10 LB]

The Bible recommends that the fellow should be restored to his or her faith by other brethren so that he or she can return to fellowship with God and man. You may check out Galatians 6:1-5.

But this in no way undermines his or her salvation, provided of course that he or she is willing to repent and return to the Lord, striving after perfection and holiness.

Wow! I am sure glad you mentioned this. Its comforting to know. You've been quite helpful.

We must thank the Lord for that.Let us share a word of prayer.

"Heavenly Father, thank you for your grace, and for your Holy Spirit which has taught us today. We come to you to say that we love you, and that by your grace we shall stay Yours until our lives' end. We know You will do anything and everything to ensure this. By your grace we shall cooperate with You and obey You all the way. Thank you for loving us so much, in Jesus name we pray, Amen."

THE END